Widower's House

Widower's House

John Bayley

Duckworth

First published in 2001 by
Gerald Duckworth & Co. Ltd.
61 Frith Street, London W1D 3JL
Tel: 020 7434 4242
Fax: 020 7434 4420
Email: enquiries@duckworth-publishers.co.uk
www.ducknet.co.uk

A catalogue record for this book is available
from the British Library

ISBN 0 7156 3076 8

Typeset by Ray Davies
Printed in Great Britain by
Biddles Ltd, *www.biddles.co.uk*

For Audi

PART I

CHAPTER ONE

Margot at Home

'Now do eat it while it's nice and hot,' ordered Margot, putting a large lump of casserole on to my plate.

I have always disliked casseroles. During our forty-four years of married life Iris and I never made a casserole. Nor did we ever eat one, except under duress, if we were guests at a dinner party.

I was tempted to say rudely that I would rather eat it nice and cold. Instead I found myself rapidly picking the largest lump off the plate – Margot at the stove had her back to me – and stuffing it into my trouser pocket.

I had never done such a thing in forty-four years of happy domestic eating, with myself usually the cook. I felt astonished by my own action: its rapidity, its pointless duplicity. Why was I behaving like this? Was it because I was different now? A different person since Iris died?

That must be it. My instinct now was to escape, to evade, to elude whatever was pressed upon me, whether it was telephone calls or chunks of casserole.

But I could not escape back into my old self, because my old self no longer existed. In widowhood you lose not only your loved one but yourself. And there was no new self to take its place. Only this indistinct creature who put the dinner pressed upon him in his pocket instead of eating it: who was an object of solicitude and a prey to the whims of kindly women.

Widowers are also full of self-pity. Intensified as it had become, this was the only recognisable trait left over from a previous personality. So I reflected in a wild way, as I manipulated the handkerchief in my pocket over the greasy lump of casserole. I used to be a different person, a person who lived with Iris for forty-four years, so different from her and so separate, and yet so completely a part of what she was, of what together we had been.

So instant is thinking that while Margot's back was turned to me as she bent over the stove – not like my stove at home – I had an infinity of time to reflect on the fact that friends, however well you know them, remain unstable and unpredictable creatures. I was wary of Margot; I was wary of her now, because I did not know what she was. She might get cross or irritable, amorous or lachrymose. Whatever she did or was would remain unknown to me. Ill or demented, Iris for me had been always the same, always 'my old cat'. She determined my being.

Well, she was gone now. I could not be the person I had been; the one who was part of her when she died of Alzheimer's disease. She had taken our two selves with her. I could see my old self clearly enough, but only as a fact of history, unrelated to what I seemed to have become.

And what was that? A new person? I did not feel in the least like a new person. Perhaps Margot was trying, even if unconsciously, to make me a new person; perhaps I was unconsciously trying to be one myself. But it didn't seem to be working. My last thought, as Margot turned back again from the stove, was that I was glad it wasn't working.

Yes, I was frightened of Margot. But that was unfair! I had known Margot for years and years. That is to say we, Iris and I, had known Margot for years and years. One of her daughters had been a pupil of Iris's, who was then teaching philosophy at St Anne's College in Oxford. The daughter was not very satisfactory as a pupil but Iris did her best, and the girl scraped a third. She was very fond of Iris, who always kept in touch with her former pupil, and helped to find her a job. Then she got married. Margot always insisted that Iris had somehow saved her daughter.

Margot took to asking us over to her house in Norfolk for the weekend. It was a long and complicated drive, which I hated. I used to try to persuade Iris to beg us out of it with some kind of excuse, but

Iris was too honest for that, and besides she felt loyalty as well as friendship for Margot. She could never resist advances, however untimely and unwanted, from people she had once helped, and who insisted on regarding themselves as pals for life. Besides, we were both genuinely fond of the big, awkward, enthusiastic woman, who combined a natural gift of goodness and kindness with being slightly comical in everything she said or did. She could be overpowering and a bit exhausting, but protected by Iris I got on with her well enough.

Her husband Guy was a great help in this. Hospitable, as garrulous as she was but unanxiously genial, he always made the going easy. I seldom got on with men as well as I did with women, but Guy was an exception. He teased and patronised me a little in a way that I enjoyed because he seemed to enjoy it; but he was always attentive and respectful with Iris, and seemed a bit in awe of her.

There was nothing much to do at their big house, and the country round about was unedifying. Their children were grown-up and we hardly knew them, except for Iris's experience of the delinquent daughter, now a model mother. Margot used to drive us to see churches which had immensely high ceilings ornamented with life-size angels. We duly exclaimed and admired; and after each church I would very much hope that we would go home to tea, or to a relaxing drink and chat with Guy. But, laughing heartily at my feeble hints in this direction, Margot used to herd us back into the car and on to the next church. Her enthusiasm had no sense of time or distance, and when we got back at last Guy would have several drinks inside him, and a box or two of Pringles.

In his time Guy had obviously made quite a lot of money, but he retired soon after we got to know them. Then suddenly and unexpectedly he died. Margot was prostrated. One year, two years later she was still a timid and uncertain shadow of herself. That was the time during which she became really close to us, or rather close to Iris. They saw each other in London, and Margot came to us as often as we went to her. Before that, she and Guy had almost always been the hosts.

I found it much easier to deal with Margot after she became a widow. Without Guy she was subdued and clinging, but easy to talk to, and always eager to be told anything that it occurred to one to tell her. We took her abroad once or twice, and that was quite a success. For a time she lost interest in her house and in the household animals to which she had once been so much attached. A cleaning lady from the village came every day to keep things tidy and to talk to her. When we visited her now, or when she came to us, we took her to the pub, where she and Guy never used to go.

After two years of disconsolate grieving she began to get over it. The improvement, I was sure, was as much due to Iris as to her family and her other friends.

When Iris began to be in the bad stages of Alzheimer's Margot was in America, staying with another of her daughters, who had an American husband. Margot got on admirably with both of them, particularly the always-hospitable husband from Virginia, and she was popular with the children too. She stayed in America for a while, and seemed quite recovered when she wrote to us, or in practice to me, for Iris by then could no longer read.

I strongly discouraged Margot from coming to see us, since I intuited that a visit might revive her own depression. Margot for once did not seem to need much discouraging. Like many naturally hearty and ebullient persons, she overflowed with sympathy for every sort of trouble, and for the trouble-prone, but she shrank from the idea of mental illness.

When Iris died Margot was in touch with me again at once, and the problem of fending her off at least distracted me from my other difficulties. But I could not manage to fend her off for long. Notwithstanding her obvious reluctance to see Iris when she was alive, Margot managed now to sound a little reproachful, however full of forgiveness. Why had I not fully owned up to my situation? Why had I not let her know? I had been a saint to look after Iris for so long and without any help, but why had I not called on her – such an old friend as she was – to come and help me? She would have dropped everything – *everything*! Surely I must have realised that?

Yes, I realised it. And I realised Margot's need for self-deception. She honestly believed – now – that she would have done these things when Iris was alive. Margot spoke more in the warmth of sorrow than with reproach, but she somehow contrived to suggest that Iris's long lapse into mental illness, and even her death, could all have been avoided if she had been on the spot herself. In the old days her busy affection and patronage had always in some way reassured Iris, however much they had flustered and sometimes irritated me. Now I felt indifferent.

But soon Margot was back on the phone. She would come to Oxford, stay as long as I wanted, help me put things in order. There must be so much to do; she knew what it was like, and of course the house had got in such a state ... In spite of the hens, the horses, the tiresome old vicar, she could leave her own house at a moment's notice.

I was sure she could. And a cold sweat started down my back at the thought of Margot in my house – our house it still was – dealing with its ageless accumulation of dust and dirt, to which, in the old days, Iris and I had both been happily indifferent. Margot would be doing the job on general principles: not censoriously, but as if, in the Duke of Wellington's words, the king's government must be carried on. There was now no one but herself to bear the white man's burden.

I managed to fight her off, but I knew that it was only a question of time before the attack was resumed. The result of the war seemed a foregone conclusion. My widower's house was already under siege. Margot was at the gates.

To continue the metaphor I won a respite by allowing Margot to open a campaign on another front. She quite understood that I might want to be alone in the house, if only for a suitable grieving period; but the weekends in particular must be so bleak and dreary now. A visit to her would make just the right sort of change. If I didn't fancy the drive, which was quite understandable, she would come and pick me up. She could do that easily.

I was sure she could. I didn't fancy the drive. Even with Iris I had always hated it. Now I shrank from travelling anywhere on my own. But I shrank just as much from the thought of having to talk to Margot in the car all the way to Norfolk.

CHAPTER ONE

When at length I capitulated, it was to say that I would drive over myself. As the dreaded day came closer I tried to find some of the shabby zip-fastener bags with which Iris and I, long ago, had been accustomed to travel. They all seemed to have disappeared from the house, as if Iris had contrived, in some miraculous way, to take them with her on her last journey.

I threw what I needed into the car, just as it was, wishing that Peter Conradi, or some other congenial friend and colleague made during the final years, would come and bear me off to France, to Africa, to the moon ... Anything to save me having to go by myself to Norfolk.

Even when Iris was ill and I had to take her on a hazardous car journey – hazardous because of the unavoidable danger of her jumping out, which she had once managed to do – her presence still managed somehow to stiffen my backbone, to lend me support as well as comfort. As a widower my only comfort now must be to stay at home.

I longed to ring Margot and tell her I was ill, unfit, couldn't possibly move. She would only have said, 'All right, I'll come to you, you poor man. Even if you're grieving you must be looked after.'

She would have known that I was not ill; but apart from that, to escape my fate was, as it were, seriously impossible.

A part of my carelessness and my indifference was a belief now in fate. To try to take the initiative from it could only lead to further trouble.

And yet I could already feel my inside beginning to dissolve at the thought of the horrors of the journey. The M25 ... those endless juggernauts, roaring on their steady note of brutish contempt as they elbowed their way past, their wheels higher than my head as I crouched in my little Fiat Panda, inches away. My stomach gave another squeeze. And the road-works and hold-ups; the confusing maze of sideways lanes on the last stretch – lanes I had travelled so often with Iris. Without her I should need more than a map to find my way there.

*

The journey was as bad as I had feared. Well, actually not quite as bad. But quite bad enough. It was a Tuesday. Margot had naturally asked me for the weekend – a long weekend she had said – but I had invented a Saturday visitor and a dinner engagement on Sunday. I had hoped in this way to postpone the inevitable to a later weekend at least – and I had devoutly hoped it would be a much later one.

Margot did not sound cross on the phone, as I had feared. Just a little more breezy. Margot could be cross, as I knew from overhearing her with her younger daughter Tamsin, who afterwards married the American, and who, like Iris's former old pupil, was at that time being a bit of a problem. But she had never been cross with Guy. Nor with Iris; nor with me.

Who could ever have been cross with Iris? It would have been undignified. My own occasional tantrums of course had no dignity, but they were part of our private language and understanding and always ended in laughter, almost before they got going. And although Iris was quite unconscious of it – this of course in the old days before she was ill – I was always under her protection. At Margot's and everywhere else.

Now that protection had gone. And without it I had discovered, to my astonishment, that I instinctively feared Margot. A harassed, settled sort of fear, as fated as everything else in my present life.

This makes it sound as if Margot was a termagant, which she most emphatically was not. But just because I now felt so vulnerable I seemed to have a false recollection of moments when her voice had been raised, with a sharp edge of raillery and exasperation in it. Unfair to fear now that I might once have heard it, but so it was. My impression, that is.

'Well, if *that's* the case,' she had said, when I prevaricated with my list of made-up engagements, 'come on Monday or Tuesday, and stay the week, or longer.'

I was relieved when she sounded just breezy, not at all put out. Obviously she didn't believe a word I had said, but that didn't bother her. Or me, come to that. The game was up, however. From her tone I knew that it would be no good trying to invent further, more pressing, yet more improbable engagements. It would be indecent even to try.

As I drove, quaking with what seemed the same kind of anxiety I knew so well from Iris's Alzheimer's, I knew that the Margot situation, for which I was helplessly bound, summed up all my widower's problems. *All old friends were now threats.* They were aimed purposefully at me; sure sources, not of reassurance, but of danger and discomfort. And out of the ground had sprung up, like the dragon's teeth, a fresh and hitherto unknown host of kind good persons, well-intentioned persons, who wanted to make life nicer and less lonely for me.

What a shit I was, or had become! But more and more, these days, I had begun to suspect that I always had been one. Widowerhood just seemed to have brought it out, like nettlerash.

Memories should always be spontaneous. But as I drove fearfully along I tried to cheer myself up by thinking deliberately of a *good* car journey, one long ago with Iris. Even towards the end of Iris's life such journeys could be good to remember, if the memories came of themselves. The best used to come when I was lying in bed in the morning beside Iris, with her tranquilly asleep at last after a busy, Alzheimer-distracted night.

During it she would have been off downstairs at two or three o'clock. I would hear her rattling the front door, always locked on the inside. Sometimes she would cry out in what could sound like indignation, although she was never indignant or in the least angry with me if I groped my way downstairs and tried as gently as I could to make her desist. She used to become quiet then, as if the last thing she wanted was for me to be upset or distressed, but it was always a quiet obstinacy. She would never come back to bed except by herself, and in her own time. And when she did, my thoughts could at last wander off freely, somewhere into the past.

I compelled them to wander off now, in the solitary car: but they failed to obey me or to comfort me. At last I hit on the device, of thinking about that happier and very much earlier journey.

We are sitting in the back of a car, as if with our tails wrapped round each other like the two bad mice. We are whispering together. In the front are my mother and my brother Michael, the driver. The car is Michael's, a big Rover car which even then had an old-fashioned, slightly grotesque look about it, although it had been a new model five years before. The road is almost empty, but sometimes we pass trucks with long bonnets saying LEYLAND on the side of them (it was that long ago) grinding their way up a long traverse in the Guadarrama. Occasionally my mother turns to look at us; not exactly with disapproval, but as if she would prefer us not to disturb the companionable silence of the front seats with our chatter.

My father had died the previous February; my mother and Michael, now very close, must have concluded tacitly between them that it would be better not to spend this Christmas at home. Michael must have been on leave. I fancy he was stationed in Hong Kong at the time. However it was decided, or whoever decided it, we were to drive through Spain to Gibraltar, by way of Cadiz and Seville.

We had drunk some excellent young Burgundy at a tiny and primitive restaurant where we had persuaded a reluctant mother and brother to stop on the way down through France; and I had bought a bottle to take away. At Cordoba I was developing a severe cold, and after a chilly morning in the Moorish cathedral I remembered the bottle as we drove out of town. Iris, wise girl, often carried a corkscrew in her handbag, and crouching down mouselike in the back of the car we passed the bottle from hand to hand with smothered and occasionally irrepressible giggles. But the pair in front never suspected what was going on; or if they did, they thought it undignified to mention the matter.

So, buoyed up with Burgundian courage, we persuaded them to make a lunch stop at Montilla in the sherry district. Fortunately they were cold and hungry too. We drank dark golden wine and ate fried sardines fresh from the coast. We were the only guests, and our host seemed to be inebriated in a jovial manner well before we left. Removing Michael's hat with a polite flourish, he put it on his own head and executed a sort of fandango. Michael, disarmed for once, produced a smile, and my mother actually clapped and said 'Bravo'.

She felt the Spaniards were behaving as she had imagined they might do when she was young.

There was no pleasure in remembering this scene in a solitary car on the roaring motorway. But I remembered it anyway.

… It is truth the poet sings
That a sorrow's crown of sorrow is remembering happier things.

Not only the motorway but everywhere I went was dangerous now, every person I met constituted a threat. The world was a dangerous place. I didn't believe in other people except as a source of trouble. The world had only made sense when Iris was there and I was looking after her.

And before that. Iris was doing her work, with me there, for more than forty years – real work. It was her own work, it had nothing to do with me: and I loved that. I basked in it. It was like being held in a hand. I was never aware of the supporting hand, and the hand was not aware of me, any more than God may be of his creation.

*

The horrible great curve going up to Cambridge. Distances and danger, and armies marching. Resolutely, in order to have something in my head, something too that I used to enjoy so much … Suppose that young Philip of Macedon had brought an army over to aid Hannibal? Or that the Barca faction had won ascendancy in the Carthaginian council; and instead of their leisurely half-reluctant way of making war the council had supported Hannibal in a *guerre à outrance*?

Why on earth do I go on thinking about things like this? As if history mattered, as if anything could ever have been done about it.

At the age of seven or eight I read a book called *The Young Carthaginian*. Malchus, the young man's name was, and he went to the wars with Hannibal, like a younger son sent out to fight with the Duke of Wellington in the Peninsula. Hannibal in the book seemed to me rather like Lord Baden-Powell the Chief Scout, about whom we had been given a talk by the games master. But even this was not enough to put me off Hannibal, or to spoil my image of the general who crossed the Alps and beat the Romans in three great battles ...

G.A. Henty (was it?) must have written that rather uncomfortably bracing book, published in a sturdy embossed binding of dark green cloth. He wrote many others along the same formula – *With Roberts to Kandahar, With Gordon to Khartoum*. Rome was supposed to be the right role model in those days for schoolboys, so it was enterprising of Henty to produce a young Carthaginian instead.

God, I hate driving! Marching would have been preferable. Winning a battle off the march – said to be the great test of generalship. Our English King Harold drove his army (of veteran professionals, mostly Danes) up Watling Street to York, defeated and killed the Norwegian king Haardrada, marched them back southward in four or five days and was ready to meet Duke William on Senlac hill. Two battles off the march. Maybe a mistake? Harold was an impetuous man. His impetuousness was admired and feared by the Welsh, seasoned guerrillas whom he had routed out from among their hills and valleys. If he had had the time to bring a few good South Welsh mercenary archers to the field of Hastings the result might have been different.

Or suppose Stonewall Jackson had not been killed at Chancellorsville? Better still, if John S. Mosby – a former Virginian lawyer and a genius at guerrilla warfare if ever there was one – had won the ear of Jefferson Davis and the Southern war leaders? A slave-owning millionaire before the war, Mosby was bankrupt when it ended. But he could have husbanded the troops and run rings around the Northern armies, instead of trying to fight them on their own terms, as Robert E. Lee and the rest of the West-Point-trained Southern commanders tried to do. Mosby was an inspired amateur, well aware that war could be too serious a matter to leave to the professionals.

Here – stop it! Why worry about the problems of these people? It's too ridiculous. But what else am I to do? Othello's occupation's gone.

Poor man. As a general, Othello was so good at his job. But then instead of war he embarked on the campaign of matrimony, to be utterly defeated in his very first engagement. He thought he had occupied his bride, as a legion occupies a campsite or an army a surrendered town. And the enemy turfed him out – first go.

Othello, like Hannibal, was quietly confident of his powers. He knew himself to be a good commander, as he would be a good husband to the woman who loved him. But widowers are not required to be good at anything. No qualifications needed. One can imagine that the counsellors at the job centre are most reassuring. You've lost your job – your caring job – but there's no need to find a new one. Previous experience of joblessness is not necessary. We'd rather you started entirely from scratch. You'll soon get the hang of it. Why not hire a new video every day? Or two at a time? Or try some experimental cooking for one?

And a bit later you could always go on an excursion or a cruise. 'Thank you, but I'd rather be in work.' 'Oh, having nothing to do *is* work, you know. That's what we always tell people,' say the counsellors.

Yes, I suppose it is. But looking after Iris wasn't work. It's now that everything is work. Telephoning is work. Facing people and fending them off is work. Living is work. Hard, nasty work.

Not when Iris was around. The world made sense then. I believed in it. Iris was faith and belief. And reassurance too.

Everybody nowadays is used to being alone in a car. Commonest of situations, at least in this country. About the only place you can be alone.

And I was going to be alone with Margot. For three or four days, perhaps more. The thought filled me with a panic which had nothing to do with my fear of the road or the solitude of the car. Once there had been the four of us. Guy and me, Margot and Iris. Now two of us were left.

There was something worse than that too. Would I, when it came to the point, *really even want to go home*? The thought made me too frightened even to start groaning and cursing the road, and the car, and Norfolk, and Margot. Of *course* I would want to go home! Home was my one refuge, the one place where it seemed natural and proper to be. So what was the matter with me? I must concentrate on getting through this new 'Margot solo' experience, emerge from it, get back to my own lair, my own burrow, where I would be safe again.

*

'You do the wine. It should be good. It's something Guy must have had in the cellar for years and years. Ought to be drunk up I'm sure.'

I had made a hash of opening the bottle of claret. Its label was foxed with mould and the cork had come to pieces. No doubt it would be wonderful stuff, but the thought of my Chilean red at home, and how much I still enjoyed waiting for it in the evening, and drinking it, getting up from time to time to see if there was any improvement in the thriller on TV – that thought prevented me from having any sense of Guy's wine. It might be very good; it might be dreadful. I really didn't know. But I sipped it dutifully.

'All right?' asked Margot, eyeing me with what I felt to be an unnecessary degree of solicitude.

'Superb,' I said faintly. 'Isn't it?'

'Oh, I wouldn't know,' said Margot in comfortable tones. 'I used to leave it all to Guy. He knew about wine.'

I knew what would have been Iris's reaction, although she would have sounded more warmly and more truly pleased about the wine than I had managed to do. But she had once remarked with a twinkle to an American publisher at the Connaught that good wine was completely wasted on her, and could she please just have quite a *large* amount of their House Red instead. I could imagine the publisher's worried look as he wondered whether the hotel would have such a thing as House Red available at all; and how much face he would lose with the wine waiter by asking.

The claret did indeed seem splendid after a couple of glasses – Margot hardly touched it – and I went on to be warmed and comforted by the rest of the bottle. But dinner was hard going. Short silences which would have passed unnoticed in the old days now seemed to extend themselves painfully. We had always found plenty to say in those old days, and in a sense Margot had plenty now, but what we said seemed to come with a lack of spontaneity, even from Margot herself. We were both looking for new ways of dealing with what should have been a nice old familiar situation.

Margot solved the problem by jumping up and down a lot.

'You've let it get cold,' she told me reproachfully, and she put another large lump of casserole on my plate.

CHAPTER TWO

Mella and the Mermaid

Safe back, after another nightmare journey, I thought about those days I had spent in Norfolk. It had been less bad than I feared, certainly much less strenuous. Margot had made no attempt to take me church-crawling, and there had been no social life. I was even spared the tiresome old vicar. I pottered about the garden and renewed my acquaintance with Margot's hens, to whom I had been much attached in the past. They were magnificent birds of huge size, with bright red combs, sharp yellow beaks and delicately speckled grey plumage. With the cock making unexpectedly deep and melodious noises from time to time to call his ladies around him, they strolled about on their massive legs, sometimes stopping with one claw raised to look me insolently in the eye. I was drawn to them as much as I had been in the old days when I used to tempt Iris away from her work to come and visit them with me, when we used to present them with bits of stale bread.

Margot had been pleased then by our interest in her giant hens, as well as our interest in the horses, the garden, and the conservatory flowers. But the hens had been our favourites, and I lingered in their enclosure now, partly, it must be said, to avoid Margot. Possibly she intuited this.

'I believe you love Mabel and Tim more than me now,' she said with a laugh, referring to her own favourites.

'Well of course I do,' I replied, trying to strike the necessary note of teasing affection. 'I don't presume to look as high as you.'

Margot made a *moue* but did not look best pleased. Presently she was calling me in for another dish that had to be eaten while it was nice and hot. I had the constant feeling that something more was expected of me. It was a dolorous, wearing, apprehensive feeling, which caused me now – back home as I was – to sigh heavily as I sat in Iris's revolving chair.

Why should more be expected of widowers, and what might this 'more' consist of? Hadn't one lost enough without being expected to make it up in some way, make it up to friends and to other people? It seemed highly unfair. I felt now that I was required to be *more* affectionate, *more* outgoing – more this, more that. As a reward for being allowed to stay at home? It felt like that. Here I was back at home anyway, safe and sound, thank God. I had escaped from them all; and as the thought occurred to me in that form I took a deep breath of satisfaction.

But I was doing it deliberately. Playing the part to please myself. I had to realise that. And all the more deliberately because I saw at that moment, and as it seemed between the flicker of an eyelid, the figure at the end of the passage. It was the same as the one I had seen on the drive over to Norfolk, the one who knew what I wouldn't tell myself. That I didn't *really* want to go home. Or to stay at home.

And at that moment the telephone rang.

Before I had sat down in the chair I had remembered that I ought to switch it off. But it wasn't, for once, an anxious thought. Surely I could safely give it another few minutes. All the more enjoyable when I turned it over, pressed the lever, and knew that no one could bother me. No sound. Just a small red light pulsing away almost invisibly on the dial.

There was no need for me to answer it. No reason. But at once I knew I would have to do so. All my pleasure in being back at home vanished into a vortex of unspecifiable fears and anxieties. Who was it? What did it want? How soon could I get rid of it? To pick up the receiver and answer the phone became an absolute compulsion. That foreboding figure at the end of the passage – a figure who might have come out of one of those cartoons in the *New Yorker* – seemed to nod in agreement, or approval.

I picked up the receiver and made a vaguely helloish noise.

'It's Mella.'

This was extraordinary. Mella had never rung me before. I had a panicky sensation that either this was Margot checking up on me, or that Mella herself was checking to find whether Margot was present, had been present, or could be about to arrive. A 'spoiling manoeuvre' of some sort, as might be said in army circles. But Mella did not know Margot, had never even heard of her!

Long ago, before Iris was ill, Mella's supervisor in another college asked me if I would take her for a few sessions on the Russian authors. She had a particular interest in them, although they only indirectly connected with the subject of her thesis. I saw her. She seemed a nice person, full of enthusiasm but remarkably ignorant, even, so far as I could see, of the English authors she was supposed to be working on. That was not so unusual, however, in students who were studying for their DPhil.

Mella loved the idea of writers and writing, rather as I like the idea of battles in the past and the generals who fought them. Dostoevsky was for her what Hannibal was for me: a glamorous figure she admired from a distance. On the other hand it is possible to find out a great deal about Dostoevsky or Tolstoy, while only very little will ever be known of Hannibal. Mella preferred to know very little of her hero; and I soon gave up trying to enlarge her knowledge.

But she continued to come and see me. She was easy to get on with. She popped her head round my door every two or three weeks, saying, 'Is this a good moment?' She was good at intuiting moments of vacancy in my college office, when I was quite glad to have a chat. At the time I was getting on for retirement anyway, and had not a great deal to do.

She liked to talk about poems or stories I had recommended, short-winded things, which she read slowly, but with great care. (I soon discovered that her real trouble, like that of a lot of students today, was the inability to read reasonably fast while taking in what was read.) She knew no Russian, but flattered me by wanting to hear bits of Pushkin in the original. She listened to these with shining eyes, and it is true that Pushkin does sound wonderful, even if you are not understanding him. But on the whole Mella preferred to talk rather than to listen, and this always suited me.

Although we were getting to know each other I heard very little about her background. I once expressed a mild interest in her name. Even that she seemed reluctant to say much about. She had been christened Melanie because her mother had loved the film *Gone with the Wind*, but her father preferred Melissa, and so she got the nickname Mella, which stuck. She was reticent, and I never asked her anything. I had always found it better in the long run if one did not know much about pupils.

She had flat, straight hair, obviously self-cut; her face was plain but pleasant, and so was her low voice which had a sort of soft wrinkle in it, sounding vaguely foreign. She had a husband or partner, it was not clear which, with whom she was not at present living, and a child with her, a small boy. He seemed of an independent turn, for his presence in her life did not, by inference, greatly discommode her. It remained uncertain whether he had been sired by the husband or partner, or was the result of some previous connection. I had no idea of her age. She might be in her early thirties; she might be older. I became accustomed to her visits. Indeed we got so used to each other that she often got up from her chair and wandered round my college room, peering at the books and talking in her vague way, sometimes stopping to look down at me in my chair.

When Iris's illness was diagnosed I gave up going into college, and I could not manage any more to see the occasional pupils whom I had been taking in retirement. I had a note of awkward condolence from Mella, offering help. I declined as politely as possible, as I had done to most other people. It was not help that was needed for Iris, but little bits of social amusement; and, perhaps mistakenly, I did not see Mella as being much good in this role. I did not like the idea of Mella coming to the house, and perhaps getting into the habit of dropping in as she used to do in college. She might even have brought her little boy, whom I had never seen and was reluctant to meet. This was bad of me, as poor Iris, in the childhood twilight of Alzheimer's, had become quite interested in children, as if they were equals or even friends.

In fact Mella at this time dropped out of mind. Not altogether out of sight, however. Two or three times a week I used to take Iris down in the car to the college to pick up my mail. It gave us something to do. Iris sat in the car and the gardener often stopped and chatted to her. He was a bachelor who kept pet rabbits. She loved hearing about these, and they got along very well together.

I came back from the lodge one day to find Mella talking to Iris, who had got out of the car. For some reason Iris never escaped on these little trips, as she sometimes did from the house if I forgot to lock the door. So I was not perturbed. She was enjoying her chat with Mella, and Mella herself had an animation, a charm even, which I had never witnessed or suspected before. Her sallow face was rather flushed, and she was lifting her hands as if to demonstrate something to Iris, who was as much absorbed in Mella's presence as a child might be who had found an adult with whom speech could be had on equal terms. I heard Mella say, 'You are a darling, Iris, I am so glad to have met you,' and then she turned quickly to me with a look of slightly guilty apology. I hastened to thank her, as a parent might thank a stranger who had shown kindness to his small son or daughter. Mella stooped awkwardly almost to the ground as if she were addressing a real child, and took Iris's hands. Iris bent down and kissed her, putting both hands against her cheeks. Murmuring something and smiling at me, Mella rose and departed as if on cue, and Iris took a few steps after her.

After this I could not but feel that I should thank Mella and ask her to come and see Iris again. But there was a difficulty. I had no idea of Mella's address or how to get in touch with her. In the past she had simply turned up, and it had never occurred to me to ask how or from where. I might have asked the don who had originally asked me to see Mella, but he had gone off to a job at another university – so long had it been since Mella first started coming to see me.

In any case Iris's condition rapidly worsened about this time, and as Mella did not appear again in the college she dropped once more out of mind. But after Iris's death I started to go back into college, where I found a big elaborate card from Mella expressing the usual sympathy and condolence.

But this card also featured a mermaid by John Waterhouse, done in late Pre-Raphaelite style, with great attention paid to the sea person's white shoulders and bosom and her long auburn hair, which she was combing with a piece of coral. She had a pensive faraway look, and the card, as its small print discreetly informed the purchaser, was delicately scented.

It was an odd choice for a condolence card, and yet I found it obscurely satisfactory, even comforting. The mermaid looked thoughtful, sympathetic, kind and good. She was doubtless Waterhouse's favourite model; and, attractive as she was, probably his mistress too. I hoped he had been in a position to be able to reward her adequately. She looked as if she might well have an impoverished family in the background, the proper maintenance of which was her chief concern. Her tail was wrapped neatly around her, and the artist had taken a lot of trouble to suggest realistically the transition of fish scales, in ascending order of size, to just below her waist. Her pubic scales, as one might call them, led the eye pleasantly into an ample and shapely white stomach, ornamented with a neat human navel.

I propped her on the kitchen table and pondered her with a melancholy pleasure, which seemed in keeping with her own subaqueous mood. How solemnly, but how engagingly too, the later Pre-Raphaelites combined sexual fantasy with a meticulous realism! I didn't particularly want to be reminded of Mella by the mermaid, but I remained intrigued by her choice of card. People, women especially, don't choose such things at random. What was the mermaid's significance in terms of Mella's now inevitably changed relationship to myself? Was she preparing to undergo a sea-change for my sake?

In the mood I then was in I didn't bother to excuse to myself the empty vanity of the conceit. Why shouldn't I, at this wretched moment, indulge myself in any comfort, no matter how puerile, that I could get hold of? I felt that the mermaid, pensively drawing the coral comb through her long tresses, would fully understand.

But at this moment, Mella, it seemed, was determined that I should

be reminded of her. While she was alive, even in the grip of Alzheimer's, Iris had protected me, just because she was being looked
after by me. A firm bulwark, she had stood between me and the people
who wanted to help us. Now that I was alone in the world it was more
difficult by far to resist encroachment. Could I be surprised from
under the sea, drawn down into those new depths? The mermaid
might be more comely, but in a curious way her features had a
resemblance to Mella's. Had Mella been aware of that?

Mella and her mermaid. They embodied in themselves the condition
of being without Iris. I heard Iris's voice from long, long ago, from
the time just after we had become 'cats' to ourselves, in our own happy
little mythology, saying 'Wow Wow.' Sometimes, if I was feeling low
for some reason, it would have a tender note and become 'Nom Nom.'

Iris's voice spoke to me still, but it could not protect me, even from
myself. I longed to escape now from Mella and her mermaid – they
were a new and alien life from which I instinctively shrank away – but
where was I to escape to?

I picked up Mella's card, and with some difficulty, because it was
stiffly and expensively made, tore it across and then across again, into
four pieces. I dropped them into the overflowing waste-paper basket.
Iris's voice sounded upset but unreproachful, as it sometimes used to
do if I had been thoughtless and bad. Mella had kissed her and been
good to her. She had not tried too hard, and been unnatural, as most
strangers unused to it became when coping with mental invalids. Iris
and she had responded to one another with perfect simplicity, as if
they had been the two children dancing together in that picture by
Breughel of the winter *kermesse*. In fact Mella was more like that child
than she was like her mermaid.

*

'I don't want to pester you,' faltered Mella.

There was such a contrast between the way she spoke now, and her
voice and manner a few months before when she had talked to Iris
beside the car, that I could not help being touched.

'That's all right,' I said, trying not to sound ungracious, and I made a vague movement as if to invite her through the door. Mella had never been to the house before. I had always been careful to avoid that. 'You said you might call in when you rang me up,' I added uninvitingly.

Mella held a done-up paper parcel in both hands, turning it awkwardly from side to side.

'This is for you,' she said.

She stood looking into the inside of the house over my shoulder. Then she gazed at me with an unnerving mixture of proprietorship and humble appeal, as if she owned me now but still looked up to me from afar.

'Come in.'

Mella shook her head slowly, with an air of knowing far more about what was wrong with me and the situation than I did. She held out the parcel again. It was clumsily wrapped, but there was no clue as to what might be in it. I could hardly thank her for it adequately without knowing what was inside, but I was determined not to start the business of unwrapping it. That would be to ask for trouble. I should never get rid of her.

Mella looked at me expectantly, and then at the parcel. She moistened her lips with her tongue.

I started to say thank you again, but she interrupted me.

'It's awful, isn't it? I know ...'

I was not going to invite explanation. I felt possessed with resolve at last. The more so as Mella had now taken a step forward, and her foot was through the door in the way that debt-collectors are supposed to behave.

'It's extremely good of you to come,' I said. 'But I'm just going out, and I do have rather a lot to do.'

Mella looked horribly understanding and forgiving. Her look was the same as Margot's had been, when she implied that if her own advice had been taken, and her supervision accepted, Iris would still be alive and well.

'I know,' Mella repeated. 'I've been through …' and again she broke off.

To a sensitive and understanding person like myself it should clearly not be necessary to say what she'd been through: nor did I wait to hear more. I joined her over the threshold and pulled the door firmly shut behind me, so that Mella had to step hastily backwards.

Revenge of a widower. Feeling as nasty as Genghis Khan I walked rapidly to the car, unlocked it, started it up with some difficulty, and prepared to back out of the gate. I waved vaguely towards Mella, and then noticed that she was still holding the parcel, which was now looking even more dishevelled. What was I to do? Stop and take it from her? I couldn't bear the thought. I backed hastily out into the road, narrowly missing a pedestrian on the pavement, waved behind me and drove off.

I took the first turning, drove around at random for a bit, and returned the opposite way round the block.

Mella was still standing outside the house, holding the parcel, waiting patiently for me to return. That was what it looked like. She would wait there for ever to give me what she had brought. I drove on down the road without pausing, peering to the left as if trying to identify a house number. I drove to college and spent a long time going through my condolence mail, which was still arriving. I even answered a couple of letters. It must have been well over an hour before I cautiously re-entered my road from the blind end. Mella was gone.

Instead of relieved I felt woebegone, as if I had been abandoned. On the way back I had worried about that wretched parcel. It made a perfect excuse for Mella to return at any moment, to present it to me all over again. Now I felt that I wanted her to come back, as soon as she liked. I had behaved shabbily. I might at least have asked her in for a cup of tea. But at the thought of getting the tea, and finding a biscuit, and making conversation with Mella at the same time, I was glad I hadn't.

I must cling to my conviction – it seemed more than mere experience – that only home was real. Mella and Margot were like phantoms of harassment, Chinese shadows as the Russians call it, flitting to and fro on a backdrop of speeches that I didn't want to hear, and appearances that intimidated instead of relieving me.

But widowers' convictions seemed as light as lovers' vows. How often had I had this same thought, and clung to it, only to realise with a sinking of the heart that I didn't *want* to be at home: that I didn't *want* to be myself, as myself now was ...

I locked the little Fiat and walked slowly over to the front door. The parcel was humbly nestled on the doorstep, as though trying to get in. That was a relief. At least I needn't expect the imminent arrival of Mella, come back to deliver her present.

I took the parcel indoors, laid it on the kitchen table, and began to undo it. I felt I must get that over as soon as possible, so as to be ready to thank Mella, on the doorstep and not beyond, the next time she came round. For come she would. I was resigned to that; and something inside me, as I very well knew, was positively looking forward to it. I secretly needed her next visit. The disingenuousness of widowers.

The parcel might look insecure and untidy, but it was a long job to get it open. The outside was held by string; inside was a stout layer of newspaper, stuck down with many lengths of Sellotape. I began to swear under my breath as I tore it; finally I fetched the kitchen scissors and treated the whole thing as Alexander did the Gordian Knot.

There was a plastic bag, and inside that, under more layers of greaseproof paper, was a large round pork pie.

I looked with interest at the pages of newspaper. It was the *Independent* of a few days previously. Just the sort of anxious, caring, well-intentioned paper that Mella would read. That started me thinking gloomily about the days, long ago, with Iris at Steeple Aston, when the *Sunday Times* and *Observer* had been delivered outside the door, early every Sunday morning. I had so much enjoyed bringing them in, and looking at the front and the back pages as I got breakfast. Iris would already be working upstairs, and she seldom bothered to look at the papers, although she liked me to read bits to her in the course of the day, or to tell her if there was anything in them about animals or fish or birds. They were a treat, the Sunday papers of those days, because we never ordered a daily paper. I never got them now, I consciously shunned them, but I missed them all the same.

Having finished reading Mella's newspaper wrapping (there was some rubbish in it about the under-fives needing counselling), I turned my attention to the pie. I was relieved it was not a cake or pastry Mella had made herself. Somehow I knew by instinct that she was no cook. This was a fine pie, bought at a thoroughly superior shop, a large and handsome pie. It must have been expensive.

Why, of all other possible things, practical things, had Mella decided to buy it for me? I was not ungrateful. It looked as if I should really enjoy eating that pie, and eating it over several days. But there was something too that Mella's bizarre present reminded me of. What was it?

Then I remembered. And how could I have forgotten? It was the Great Pie – and this one might have been its twin – which Iris and I had once bought and brought home. It had been laid on the kitchen table, and when I went up to Iris, working in her study (it was a Saturday) and suggested some lunch, we came down full of expectation. A slice of that noble pie, crisp yet moist, jellied and rich but homely in texture, was just what we wanted. Perhaps with half a tomato and a leaf of lettuce.

The pie was not on the table. We must have left it in the plastic bag with the other things we had bought. We must have put it somewhere else: in the fridge, in the cupboard; there were so many other places where we might have put it. We were not unduly perturbed. It would be bound to turn up in a minute or two.

But it didn't. We searched everywhere. We began to get quite cross: with the shop, with the pie, with each other. It must have rolled out of our bag somehow; or the shop man must have taken it back by some sleight of hand, and charged us for it while retaining his pie. We would never go to that shop again, but what shop was it? We had already forgotten. In the heat of our disappointment I even accused Iris of removing the pie herself and beginning to eat it surreptitiously upstairs. To this base charge she very properly made no reply beyond a dignified but forgiving look. But she searched harder than ever, peering on her knees again and again into the same crowded frowsty shelves and cupboards, full of nameless bulging cardboard boxes and old frying pans with greasy interiors. In such places the pie might have lurked undiscovered for ever.

And so it must have done. It was never seen again. And here came Mella, months after Iris's death, bearing an identical pie, offering it humbly as a gift. Iris and I had soon recovered, and 'Gone to Pieland' became a myth and a joke, a mode of exorcising the many things that must be somewhere or other in the house, but had never reappeared.

The pie had come back at last. Too late. I felt I should not want to eat it. But I did of course – or started on it – the next day. And very good it was.

Mella had certainly come back into my life. And yet she did not reappear. Perhaps she had received the message that I did not want to be called on at home? It had never struck me before that she had a sensitive soul – rather the contrary. In college, when she had wanted to come and see me, she came. When she wanted me to tell her something, when she wanted to bore me with some idea of her own that she fancied, she came and inflicted herself on me without hesitation. In those days I came to quite like being bored by Mella.

The pie lasted me nearly a week and showed no tendency to disappear. Every time I had a slice I wondered where Mella had got it, and where she was. I couldn't write to thank her; I had no idea of her address. Days passed. Sensations of missingness, even of guilt, did not pass. They increased with the simultaneous emptiness and clutter inside the house. And once again the familiar ghost in my head, of Iris's voice and phrase – 'Woof Woof Nom Nom' – became more frequent, and more clear. Iris seemed glad, too, that the Great Pie had come home at last.

In those days the TV reached rock-bottom. Even in late evening there were no good murders, hauntings, shootings, kidnappings, car chases … No horror. Only insipid rubbish about disturbed families, rock stars, inane competitions. I never fell asleep over the supper table now; and if I tried drinking more wine than my usual more-than-adequate amount it began to taste disagreeable.

The fact was that I was now missing Mella. I had behaved badly. I had implied all too clearly that I didn't want to see her, and she had received the message. I began to feel quite sorry that she had.

Mella reappeared one afternoon on the doorstep, just as she had done the previous time. I went to the door hoping it would be her and hoping it would not be. When I saw her I realised that I was not disappointed. I welcomed her in quite warmly and suggested a cup of Nescafé. It was easier than tea.

'Oh, that would be a nuisance. It would be a bore for you, and I know you don't like me to bore you. But as you liked the pie I've brought you another one.'

I could scarcely believe my ears. Even more disconcerting than Mella's calm assumption that I had liked the pie was her comment about boring me, and the knowledge that it showed. I could feel my face going red and I blinked rapidly several times. But I managed to speak.

'How did you know I liked the pie? You're quite right, I did. But I couldn't write to thank you because I didn't know your address.'

'I'll give it to you some time. I was sure you liked the pie, because I could feel you wanting to write and thank me. I'm telepathic that way,' said Mella with a small laugh that seemed to want to give the impression of shyness and timidity, but failed to do so.

I had a vision of the future in which Mella would wing her way to the house from time to time, like one of Elisha's ravens, a pie in her beak.

'You must let me pay,' I said, in an effort to keep matters on a formal basis. 'Those pies must be very expensive. But I really am grateful. They're so very good.'

'No, they're not cheap,' said Mella with pride, as if she had been buying such pies all her life, 'but I think a man needs something meaty. And so easy. No cooking.'

All this was quite unlike Mella's usual way of going on. It was disquieting too. If a man needed a pork pie he probably needed other things, which Mella, in her new proprietary guise, might feel herself well able to supply. Quaint and even touching as this new persona of hers might be, I was not at all sure I liked it. It was like a threat hanging over my head. There seemed something slightly German about it. I remembered the round rosy face of Hannelore, the girl I had known when I was stationed in Germany after the war. She, too, had been shy but proprietary, impregnably respectable, but also giving the impression that she well knew what men liked. '*Mein Mann*, who needs his pork pie.'

These disquieting thoughts and recollections went through my mind as I filled the kettle and put a spoonful of coffee in a mug. Mella looked hungrily on as if she were itching to perform these offices herself.

'Aren't you going to have a cup?' she said.

I told her, untruthfully, that I had just had one before she came. I felt it wiser to isolate Mella's coffee drinking; it shouldn't seem to be mutual, a family affair.

Entering a friend's house they've never been into, some people look round them with frank curiosity, taking in the decor, appraising the pictures and the furniture. Others, the more diffident or better-mannered majority, seem to take no notice until social relations with host or hostess are well under way. Then interest can be shown and compliments paid.

I was relieved to see that Mella belonged to this second group. I had no interest in the house myself nowadays, and I hardly noticed the state it had got into, but I most certainly did not welcome any brisk and disorienting renovation on the part of a female well-wisher. I had a comforting sense that at least Mella was not one of the sweeping and garnishing brigade.

If anything were to be done to the house it would have to be radical, even revolutionary. A series of new times, as Dryden had put it in his poem, would have to begin.

A revolution? Would it start with one of the two women who now seemed to be playing a major part in my life, and if so which one?

*

As I watched Mella drinking her Nescafé and beginning to chatter away in something like her old style, I thought of Margot, and what her impact on my domestic scene might be like. For some time now she had been ringing up to say she must come and visit me. Drop by, as she put it. I viewed the threat of her arrival with mixed feelings, as I viewed Mella's unheralded arrivals with pork pies. How long would it be before both women had a foot in my door?

And how would I feel about that? A few weeks before I should undoubtedly have viewed the prospect with unmixed dismay. It went clean against my instinctive wish, now that I was alone, for a quiet, solitary, self-centred life-style, with its own official and acknowledged sadness; and its own private pleasures and routines. Boredoms and anxieties too of course; but at least they would be boredoms and anxieties of my own, to be dealt with in my own way, just as the pleasures and rewards would belong only to me, in my new kind of life.

Like all proposals for a way of living that one deliberately puts to oneself, this one was clearly not going to work just like that. I flattered myself that I saw this clearly. It would include all sorts of regrets and yearnings, as well as the plain misery of deprivation. But social engagements and events, including what I had begun to think of as 'Alzheimering', would merely confirm, however tiresome they might be, the placid rhythm of the life I had in mind for myself. I should not be faced with the nightmare of a helpless unpredictable existence, engineered and orchestrated by forces right outside my own control.

Now that both Margot and Mella looked like having a foot in my door, this quiet, sad, untroubled life seemed more than ever difficult to achieve. When I was young, and the war was going on – and in its earlier stages going very badly – my lugubrious elders often observed that if the politicians had only dealt with Hitler in time, nipped the blasted little fellow in the bud so to speak, we should not have had to fight this war. Self-evident, what? I had neither the knowledge nor the wish at the time to remark that a timid and peace-loving electorate would never have stood for such a daring line of action. Dealing with Hitler would have been like arresting a criminal because he was sure some day to commit a crime.

And well now, was there an analogy here with my position *vis à vis* Margot and Mella? A cold, calculating creature inside me was saying that I must expect a great deal of trouble from both of them, unless I nipped their overtures in the bud, dealt with them as Hitler should have been dealt with, however unlike him the two women might be. Someone else inside me, possibly more un-nasty though equally calculating, was saying: 'We are born to trouble anyway, as the sparks fly upward. Why try to avoid it, in this or any other form? You know quite well,' this part of me went on, 'that you are already finding what should be your tranquil and unoppressive widower's life is in practice a harassed, anxious and melancholy one.

'Think of those dreary Sunday evenings at home,' this inner self remorselessly continued, 'with nothing to distract you from your thoughts and memories; the same memories you used to enjoy so much when you looked after Iris, and that amiable fellow Belial brought them to comfort you every afternoon and early morning. Think above all of the Voice. Do you want to go on hearing it whenever you are low and alone?'

Yes, I knew the Voice. It belonged to a being that was not Iris. It was Memory in person, a creature that lived on human flesh and was sucking dry my blood and bones. So both parts of me agreed, like the men of Munich, to do nothing; to hope for the best while waiting to see what would happen. (No doubt vulgar curiosity played its part, too, in my own lack of decision.)

Nipping Mella and Margot in the bud would in practice have proved a far from simple operation; in fact it would have been a highly complex one. I had cause to realise this the very next morning when the phone, which I had reconnected the previous evening to take a call from America, rang at nine o'clock.

'John, I'm coming over to help you.'

'Oh Margot, not just at the moment if you don't mind. I'm rather busy.'

'That doesn't matter. I won't interfere in the least with what you're doing. But someone has just *got* to deal with the state of that house of yours. It really isn't fit for you to live in.'

'But I like living in it as it is,' I said feebly.

'I daresay you do, but it's not good for you. So let me at least come and *try* to do something. When's convenient for you?'

This was the challenge direct. I knew it. If I was firm now ... I had only to say, 'Margot, you are very kind. But kindness, even your kindness, is not what I want just at present. I want, if you don't mind, to be left here on my own.'

If I were to say that, even with yet further softening and modification, the thing would be done. All might yet be well.

Margot had always been blunt and rather clumsy about what she said and how she said it. In her it was an engaging, even an endearing characteristic. Besides, she would not take offence. She was too good a soul for that; and even if I had weakened a refusal still further by adding: 'Do come a little later perhaps, when I'm more settled in myself,' she would have obeyed, she would have bowed to *force majeure*. She would have importuned me no further. She would have said something like, 'Of *course* I understand, darling, I know just how you're feeling. Only keep me in touch, won't you, for when things get better?'

All I had to do was to exhibit the stronger will.

But the will and the telephone, in my experience, do not go together. They make bad and treacherous companions. So no doubt that was why I found myself babbling, 'Oh Margot, do come. How wonderful! I was hoping you'd ring. I've so much been looking forward to seeing you ... And hearing from you ...'

*

'I've brought you a small smoked chicken,' said Margot. 'Iris was so fond of them – do you remember?'

Well, of course I remembered. Iris was tactful. She said how good the smoked chicken was while really preferring, as I knew very well, a piece of cheese, or baked beans with tomato ketchup.

'What was the road like?' I asked.

'Perfectly *dreadful*! As usual.'

Margot's voice was exuberant. She always enjoyed her drive. She would have enjoyed driving to hell with her small smoked chicken if the Devil had been in trouble and requiring her services.

As we ate the chicken, which admittedly was very good, I thought uneasily of Mella's last visit. I devoutly hoped she would not take it into her head to come again while Margot was here. After the arrival of the second pie, for which I had insisted on paying her, there had been no sign of Mella during the last week. As she left on that occasion she said, 'You don't mind my coming to see you, do you? You must tell me if I'm being a bore.' She pronounced the word in an odd manner, a combination of 'Boer' and Russian 'Boyar', and she pro-longed it as if it were a word she was particularly proud of.

She did not give me her address. Nor did I ask for it.

I felt touched by Mella's wish not to be a bore, which in fact she never was. Besides, I rather like boring women. They are usually quite restful to listen to, whereas boring men are exhausting, and sometimes demanding as well.

I escorted Mella to the front door, which seemed the best way of seeing her off, though she was always good about not outstaying her welcome. As we reached the door she turned to me, as if impulsively, and put her hands on my shoulders, at the same time kissing me a few times on the face.

This seemed not entirely unpremeditated – perhaps spontaneous gestures rarely are. I was very touched all the same, although the moment was a shade comic as well. It seemed as if Mella was demonstrating her understanding of the male need for tangible female affection; something which the simple creatures might themselves be only partly aware of. They were greedy for it, if only unconsciously, just as they were greedy for pork pies. ('*Mein Mann hat immer Hunger.*') Mella's Germanic persona seemed much in evidence at this moment.

None the less her kindly gesture set alarm bells ringing all over my nervous system. I tried to look pleased but also rather wry and sad, as if my widower's status had quite retired me from the arena of the passions. Or the appetites even.

And what would be Mella's next move? Was she methodically

coming closer to me by trenches and parallels, like the besiegers of Uncle Toby in *Tristram Shandy*? As an old soldier, Uncle Toby knew all about that.

Tristram Shandy was not a reassuring precedent. Uncle Toby himself was a bachelor, under siege by the widow Wadman, so our positions were in a sense reversed. I was a widower under siege. I recalled that Sterne's old soldier became resigned to the prospect of his matrimonial fate, but could not help feeling wistful when he thought of the pleasure of lying diagonally across the bed, a position he would have to renounce when united with his bride. And it struck me that I, too, was getting quite fond of the experience of having a whole bed to myself with plenty of room to wander about and find a cool patch if one side became too warm.

Now alarm bells of all sorts were certainly ringing. There came back to my mind a comic postcard, which a facetious colleague sent me shortly after I became a professor. A mild little zoologist is examining bugs with a magnifying glass somewhere in the jungle, with his female assistant ready to write down his findings in her notebook. An enormous and very cheerful-looking monkey hangs above her from a tree and places his huge paws over her well-developed bosom, while she, her eyes on the page and unaware of what is going on, remarks good-naturedly, 'Now now, Professor – no monkey business!'

Monkey business of any sort was certainly absent from my life at the moment.

Life none the less seemed to be becoming more and more unpredictable and uncontrollable, and just in those places where it should have been simple, even agreeable, to forecast and to arrange. As Mella went away I made some gesture of farewell, and she returned the wave. I recalled with some relief that she had again said she would give me her address, but that she had forgotten to do so. Unless the forgetting was intentional.

With an effort I brought back my attention to what Margot was saying as she munched the chicken leg held between her fingers. I would have to start thinking now about how best to entertain her during her stay. To my relief she had already said she had to leave on

Friday. That meant three clear days. Looking round her with a large gesture while she drank some white wine soon after her arrival, she had announced her intention of setting about the house and making it look a *bit* better anyway. I decided I must postpone this operational plan of hers as long as I could.

As part of the postponing process I suggested after lunch that we might go and look at some of the colleges. She hadn't really seen very much of Oxford, had she? But Margot saw through that at once. It was all very well for her to drive Iris and me, as she used to do, over half of East Anglia to view the magnificent old churches. When it came to sightseeing as a guest Margot's enthusiasm seemed to have quite vanished. No, no, she would start on the house at once.

But she didn't. That was something anyway. She sat and chatted; she strolled in the garden; she spent a long time upstairs in the tiny spare room unpacking her belongings. By then it was time for an early tea, after which I suggested a little walk to Wolfson College to visit the garden and the bridge over the Cherwell. To this Margot agreed, with some appearance of pleasure, and when we came back it was time for drinks. So the day ended, quite pleasantly and without undue trouble.

Lying in bed and still sleepless I considered its events. It was the first time since Iris died that a female guest had stayed in the house, and that was vaguely disquieting; although it was quite normal, after all, and Margot had seemed to take her occupation of the spare room entirely for granted.

There was really no need to feel threatened and disquieted. No doubt widowers' weakness, as it might be called, was a well-known phenomenon in circles which widowers – and perhaps widows too – frequented. The widowers imagined, poor creatures, that women were always running after them. They misunderstood the kindness women bestowed on them in their trouble. They became inordinately vain, as if with an occupational disease. Pathetic really.

I was reassured, as I lay, still sleepless, by the growing conviction that there was really no more to it than that. Mella like Margot, Margot like Mella: the pair of them only wanted to be helpful ...

And yet at the back of my mind I couldn't help feeling that there was something helpless about their own behaviour, as if they were dismasted ships in a gale, drifting on to a lee shore. Was that too just vanity? There was certainly no evidence for the impression, beyond the sense that we all three wanted something, and that we were none of us sure what it was, or how to get it if we had been.

But naturally we all wanted something! People always did. I thought that I wanted peace and quiet. But that, too, was probably an illusion. As for what the pair themselves wanted, ever since Iris became ill other people, their motives and tastes and wishes, had become a mystery, at once complex and dull, which I had neither time nor patience to try to understand.

I ought to do better now. At least I ought to try. But I lacked any urge to start. For one thing desire, sexual desire, seemed so far away now that I could barely remember what it was like, or how terribly worthwhile and important it had once been. Even when it had only taken the form and the fulfilment of fantasy.

By evening I was feeling the strain of the day. I assembled our supper of tinned spaghetti and tinned spinach, with kipper fillets as a preliminary, and hoped that Margot would not find it too unworthy of her. Iris and I used once to love spaghetti; I made it often, but I had lost the heart to make it now. The art too perhaps.

I had put Margot in the drawing-room with a drink, but of course she kept coming in and asking whether she could do anything; looking all too critically interested, as it seemed to me, in the preparations that were going on. I thought longingly of the happy days – well, the happy if sometimes rather exhausting days – when we had been part of a well-balanced quartet, Guy and Iris absorbing and tempering the impact of Margot's personality upon the group as a whole.

Margot didn't cook in those days. She had an old retainer who had been with her for years, even before she married Guy. Ethel had been taken on by Margot's family as a Barnardo orphan of fifteen or so; and when the parents died and Ethel had been up for sale, as it were, between the three daughters of the family, there had been keen competition to retain and secure her by then invaluable services. Ethel had firmly announced her intention of 'going with Miss Margot', the youngest of the family and at the time a drama student living in Chelsea. Margot was, however, already engaged to Guy, so she was able to bear Ethel off in triumph to her new married home. Ethel stuck firmly to Margot for the rest of her life, never showing any disposition to marry or have children of her own. When she died she was greatly missed by Margot and Guy and their children, and indeed by Iris and me too.

I had sat Margot down on a reasonably clean chair in the drawing-room and got her a Bell's whisky with some tapwater. Naturally I remembered the drink she had always had in the old days. Equally naturally I gave careful thought to our supper, but I doubted that Margot would think much of it, although she would affect to be fascinated by its novelty. Clearly I could not match the shepherd's pie or the steak-and-kidney pudding that Ethel used to make, nor had I anything for afterwards to rival her rice pudding or her treacle tart – a particular favourite of Iris's.

After Ethel died Margot made no attempt to find another 'treasure'; nor did she try to do much cooking herself. But she was the kind of masterful and magnetic woman who has no trouble in getting things done for her and finding people to do them. Persons of both sexes rushed to make cakes and pâté for her, put the car to rights, prune the rose bushes. She had the knack of combining authority with mateyness in just the right proportions.

Even before Guy died Margot barely bothered with cooking. When we were there she sometimes made pasta which was short on cheese, to say nothing of garlic and olive oil. And yet the myth persisted among all her friends that Margot was a wonderful cook. She was careful not to dispel this myth by giving a dinner party. After Guy died she gave up entirely and lived as we did on odds and ends. The casserole she made for me on my first evening in Norfolk was a one-off display of welcome.

Dinner tonight was not too unsuccessful, and afterwards we watched television, to which Margot, strangely enough, was wholly unaccustomed. Although the mildest of men, Guy had always declined with some acerbity to have one in the house, and it may have shown how much she missed him that Margot had neither the heart nor the will to get one after he died.

The channels were all equally wretched that evening, and Margot watched with a kind of sorrowful and incredulous attention, as if barely able to believe that such nonsense was possible in the last year of the millennium.

I did not sleep well – nothing unusual in that these days – and I was glad when morning came, though I now had to wrestle with the problems of Margot's breakfast. Would she want it upstairs, in bed? Formerly I used to assemble toast and honey and her pot of Lapsang, and either Iris or I would take it up to her. But Margot solved the problem by appearing herself only a few minutes after eight, and bustling about the kitchen, demanding where things were kept.

This threw my morning into a state of confusion from which it barely recovered. Immediately after breakfast Margot demanded the whereabouts of the Hoover. I could not remember myself, but it must be somewhere among the confusion of macintoshes, plastic bags and cardboard boxes which filled the cubbyhole under the stairs. I unearthed it eventually and Margot eyed it with disfavour. But when I got it going she seized it at once and pushed it vigorously over the floor, exclaiming unnecessarily about the terrible state the carpets were in, and requesting me to get out of the way as I followed her about.

Quite soon the machine was in grave difficulties, like an old person called upon to perform a feat far beyond his physical strength. It still roared away impotently but it was obvious that it was not doing its job. I switched it gratefully off and Margot advised me to have it seen to properly or, better still, to buy a new one. After that she seemed to lose interest in the state of the house, for which I was equally grateful.

At my suggestion we went out to lunch. After the Hoover debacle it was easy to persuade Margot; and afterwards she showed a surprising and rather touching interest in the local shopping facilities. I was now beginning to feel more at home with her in my role as a comparatively new widower. She seemed so happily oblivious of whatever anxieties and worries I might be feeling about the problem of entertaining her. She was wonderfully unworried and serene, as if she had no sense of what any other person might be thinking and feeling. How restful her husband must have found this trait! And now I, as widower, was getting the benefit of it from his widow!

How restful it would be for me to be with her, once I had grasped this new and elementary point, which had never occurred to me when Iris was alive and we had visited Margot, or been visited by her. Now I realised that she simply didn't notice me, or pay me attention.

Margot's three-day stay went really very well. In any case, any change from the Norfolk house, which would, I realised, feel large and lonely now, must in the nature of things be some sort of relief. What we chiefly did together, without speaking of it, was to organise getting through the day; I had been long enough in the business to know that this simple fact was what mattered most. I was bound to feel a secret comradeship with Margot, just in this matter of passing the time.

To my relief she did not attempt, after that first encounter with the Hoover, to come to grips with the house-cleaning problem. After the first morning she seemed to accept its original state as naturally as I did myself. On the last night we both drank a lot of my red Bulgarian and sat chatting in the kitchen until it was quite late. We went comfortably to bed, and for once nowadays I soon fell asleep.

I woke abruptly, feeling unaccountably displaced. The night was very black, and it felt cold too, so that my impulse was to burrow closer down under the duvet. Something seemed to be there, a large presence in movement; and then a voice close to my ear whispered not to worry: go to sleep.

Sleep was the last thing that seemed possible at such a moment. A bulky form nudged me tentatively, and then settled down against me like a piece of soft cargo released by the derrick and bedding down into its position in a ship's hold. I had just begun to grasp what was going on when Margot gave a heave, and her voice started whispering again in my ear.

'Don't mind my being here, Johnny. I couldn't sleep for some reason, and I thought this might be comforting for both of us. Sleep is the thing now, I feel, don't you?'

I did. But how was it to be arrived at in the present circumstances? I was overwhelmed by conflicting sensations, the main one, I'm sorry to say, being regret that our relations, which seemed to have settled down in such a comfortable way, would now be fatally disturbed. I felt touched by what Margot had said about this being comforting for both of us – she must miss Guy's presence in the bed in the same animal way that I missed Iris's – but just at the moment it was not easy to agree with her. Also I did not care for being called Johnny, although Margot had sometimes called me that affectionately in the past, when the four of us had been together.

Thinking all these things simultaneously I remained as immobile as a spider trapped in an empty bath and uncertain in which direction to run. Margot's ample presence, now that she had settled down, was indeed comfortable rather than the reverse, but not exactly comforting. It had been restful to be with her during the last three days, because she had seemed contented herself, and unaware of me. She continued to whisper in my ear, her voice husky and penetrating; and from what she said, it seemed she had been very far from unaware. She had been thinking about me in relation to herself. And why not, after all?

She was saying now how wonderful the last three days had been; how we must spend more and more – much more – time together. We were both lonely people now, weren't we? We could do so much to help each other. I could do so much to help her; and she hoped, she did hope, that I would let her do the same for me. She knew she could.

All this was so unlike what had seemed our happy obliviousness of each other (for Margot's of me had soon produced a corresponding ability in myself to take her for granted) that I could only reflect despondently on the transformation that seemed to have overtaken us. Margot seemed all too conscious of me now as a body to clutch and a mind to be reconnoitred and invaded. From her, as she now was, I could only want to escape: and this was hardly practicable when it was three in the morning and we were lying in bed together.

47

There was an even more urgent problem to be considered. Would Margot later on expect me to – well, *do* anything? In fact to make love to her? Lying comfortably against me as she was, and continuing to whisper into my ear, made any such expectancy on her part seem, for some reason, less likely. The question could at least be postponed. And gradually I became aware that the whispering sounds – to which I had hardly been attending, so absorbed was I in my own mental activity – had been replaced by regular breathing, with an occasional mild snore.

What a relief that was! I could only admire her quite passionately for being able to go calmly off to sleep in such tricky circumstances. Or perhaps they were tricky only for me? Perhaps my comfortable relation with Margot could be resumed tomorrow without as much difficulty as I had feared.

I must have been soon asleep myself. And we slept late. I opened my eyes to see I was looking through Margot's hair, with which my face was lavishly entwined. In the daytime Margot's hair was wound up in an artfully copious bundle on top of her head. This must be why I had never noticed it before.

Spread out now on the pillow it presented an arresting spectacle. Most of it was more or less black, some of it dead white, the two shades not combining but contrasting in separate strands and locks.

Margot at this moment gave a little groan and turned her head. The hair on the pillow followed it in a slightly unnerving manner.

'I was just admiring your hair,' I hastened to say, to gain time.

Very adroitly, considering that she was half asleep, Margot seemed to take the hint, and what it implied. In these highly unusual circumstances I was asking for help. I wanted to be given a lead.

'I can't bear dyed hair,' she said. 'Of course it's going white hand over fist, but that's better than having it purple or something.'

I was glad to see that she was wearing a serviceable flannel nightdress, dark blue in colour.

The cue that Margot had so promptly followed had, I now realised, been what she was going to do anyway: that is to say, to be exactly as she had been for the last three days. She got up and went off to the bathroom, and at breakfast-time we were just as easy together as we had been before the night, about which nothing was said.

I had a feeling about her which was new to me, and which in its own way was very cheering, although I don't know why I should have had such a feeling at this point. Margot, I felt, had lots of things going on, people she saw and the problems of such people, with which she helped them cope.

Even a lover maybe? I was one among others. It was hard to say why this realisation should have come to me at the moment it did, but so it was. What had happened in the night had not been so important after all. Margot had only wanted to be kind.

CHAPTER THREE

Comédie Française

There is nothing like the departure of a guest after a successful visit for making a widower feel happy and tranquil when left on his own at home. The morning stretched before me, lazy and angelical. I would sit about for a while, look at a book, stroll into the garden (it was a balmy sunlit morning), walk out to the shops, choose my own time to have a leisurely lunch with a certain amount to drink. Perhaps a short nap to follow, for sleep last night had been rather patchy, to say the least ... A calm tranquil day. A real widower's day. I contemplated it with satisfaction.

The doorbell rang.

Probably the postman or a special delivery. Tiresome, but not threatening. I went to the front door.

When Mella saw my face her mouth seemed to turn down at the corners. Seeing this I readjusted it – my face – and wondered what line to take; while the delectable, quiet day I had looked forward to receded like a mirage.

'Isn't this a good moment?' asked Mella anxiously.

If I said no, she would go away, and I would feel unhappy about it, and the day would be spoilt anyway.

'Of course it is. Come in.'

As if she had been waiting for this invitation to perform a small but necessary duty Mella made an awkward little swoop forward to give me a kiss on the cheek. Her right to do this seemed to have been established by that 'spontaneous' gesture of affection that she had bestowed on me when we said goodbye last time.

Unable to contemplate the pleasant day I had planned I now contemplated Mella, with rather more objective interest than I had

51

done before. It was something to do with my recent experience of Margot; perhaps, oddly enough, of our having been in bed together.

Shapeless and yet slight, with her sallow skin and straight mouse-coloured hair, Mella always had the air of having been blown to my door like an autumn leaf, rather than by conscious volition. Her appearance was in complete contrast with that of Margot – dark, ample, dynamic – and yet there was a kind of resemblance between them. Both had an uncertainty about them, however little it might be apparent in Margot's case. Both could bother me by their air of looking for something, and not being sure what it was, or how to set about getting it. And both, of course, had a great deal in their lives that I knew nothing about, and wanted to know nothing about. Hadn't I had that very feeling this morning with Margot? And Mella, of course, had her little boy, and other attachments too: a husband or partner, boyfriend, whatever you called them.

And I? Didn't I have attachments? Well no, I didn't, not any longer. And that was the problem, or the danger. I was the vacuum they seemed to be drawn into, however occupied with other matters they might be. I was the lee shore on to which they might be drifting.

Mella was looking at me rather anxiously. I had probably been staring at her without seeing her for quite a little while. I hastened to offer her usual Nescafé and chocolate digestive biscuit.

'Oh, you darling,' said Mella, rather unnecessarily I thought, and she kissed me as if formally on both cheeks.

I was amused by the kiss, and pleased and touched too. I knew that Mella was conscientiously copying what people did nowadays in ordinary social situations, among friends. The habit wasn't by any means universal. And yet Mella intuited that this was what I did with other people, other friends, and so she wanted to do it to me too. Yet there seemed to be something unnatural about her this morning, which made me feel uneasy in my turn.

Questing about as she often did nowadays, Mella was now well into the main confusion of the house. But then I saw her stop like a bloodhound, stiffen and look about her as if she had scented the presence and the activities of someone else. Another woman? Such a possibility had never occurred to me. Margot after all had done virtually nothing to change the look of the house. Once the Hoover gave up she had abandoned it all to its state of original sin; and I was grateful that she had.

None the less Mella had sensed something from the moment she came in; and it seemed to be the scent of a threat – the subtle atmosphere of another woman's proprietorship. Was this why she had kissed me? As if to make her own formal claim?

Wasn't that really a bit absurd? Surely women nowadays did not feel automatic jealousy about other women who had strayed unknowingly into their territory? It must be just masculine conceit to suppose so. Besides, why should my house be in any sense Mella's own territory? None the less I had the uneasy feeling that this was the way in which Mella was beginning to think of it.

Without a word, after she had finished her coffee, she started to clean the kitchen windows, using some old bits of newspaper dampened in the sink. I remonstrated in vain. I weakened then, and offered her various cloths I found in the kitchen cupboard, but she told me her mother had always used an old newspaper, saying it was the best way to get a window-pane clean. I promptly asked about her mother, not because I wanted to know, but to try to stop her. She blocked that off by asking for a bucket, and things now began to move as if with their own terrifying impetus. Stalking about like an automaton Mella finished the kitchen windows and started on the ones in the drawing-room.

'Why are you doing this?' I asked her in despair, adding, 'I shall have to go out soon. I really must.'

Mella was on her knees by this time, doing something to the floor. Her meagre behind, clad in orthodox student jeans, not very clean ones, stuck out as she pushed her cloths to the full reach of her now bare arms. She had asked me for a mop, and although I told her there wasn't one so far as I knew, she had made an exhaustive search of the house and the cupboards.

'I'll bring one next time,' she said.

By now I was in a daze. How was I to get rid of her? I remembered the time she had brought the first pie, and I had got her out of the house, and she had remained standing patiently by the door, where I found the pie when I came home.

This was a far, far more serious situation. The grim determination with which she was now working seemed to make any form of intervention impossible. I hesitated.

'You go on out,' said Mella, without looking up from the floor.

'But what about you?'

'Oh, I'll just finish up and then let myself out. Don't worry.'

This was a new Mella, one I had never seen before. The sight of her, and all those grimly vigorous movements, gave me a qualm of apprehension. What on earth had happened?

'Well, if you're sure you'll be all right,' I said feebly.

I was giving in to her in the most abject fashion, and I still could not think how it had happened, and why. My one wish now was to get away. To get away from my own house! Suppose she refused to move out when I got back? What would I do then? And what about her little boy, and the girlfriend with whom she seemed to be more or less living? Alison? Angela? Some such name. Mella had told me once.

There was a vigorous, almost violent flopping and sopping sound of wet cloths. Feeling now slightly lightheaded, I fled out of the room and got to the front door. There I paused. I still could not make my mind up what to do. That happy anticipation of the day which I had had after Margot left – how many hours and ages ago? – crossed my mind like his past life before the eyes of a drowning man. I had actually shut my eyes, I found. Opening them again I saw Margot's driving gloves, lying in the most conspicuous position possible, on the little ledge by the front door. She had forgotten them.

They were a very elegant pair. Her driving gloves were one of Margot's few affectations. She always wore them, as if they were the outward and visible sign of the good driver she undoubtedly was. They were of black stringlike material, with black leather palms pierced with holes as if for better grip or aeration or something. They looked extremely expensive.

I remembered that we had stood chatting by the front door, and had continued to chat as we walked to the car with me carrying her bag. And they must be almost the first thing Mella had seen as she entered the house. No wonder she had looked round the kitchen in that questing perturbed way, as if she had been almost frightened of finding something more. She had certainly seen those gloves.

*

While she was here, Margot had two or three enormously long telephone conversations with friends or relations. She apologised for the length of these, and the expense. She even offered to pay for them, an offer which I, of course, dismissed with the usual rather exaggerated emphasis. (Suppose instead of 'Of course not – wouldn't hear of such a thing!' one were to say 'Very well. I calculate you were on the phone for an hour and a half, which would come to about eleven quid – we'll say ten. Give me a cheque if it's more convenient …'.) During one of these conversations I overheard Margot saying, 'Darling, Johnny's house is like those Augean Stables. I'll really have to do something about it.' Then she laughed heartily at something said the other end.

'You know what George said?' she told me afterwards. 'I'm afraid I told him, darling, that your house was worse than the Augean Stables and I should have to do something about it. So he said: "I suppose you had better imitate Hercules, Margot, and divert the river Cherwell through it!" He can be quite witty, old George.'

I had not met old George, whoever he was, nor did I wish to. I felt some resentment against Margot for discussing my house with him in these familiar terms. Margot often surprised me with remarks and references which seemed deliberately designed to show the wide circle of her knowledge and acquaintance.

Well, Margot had not carried out her promise, or threat. She had not done something about it. She had left the Augean Stables to Mella.

*

CHAPTER THREE

I came home at last to find Mella gone. In a cowardly way I had postponed my return to late evening. I had wandered about the town: I had even thought of going to the cinema – something I had not done for years. When I came back I left the car some distance off and approached the house as if casually, but with great caution. All was quiet. It was now twilight, but no lights were on inside. What would I have done if they had been? I could hardly bring myself to think of the horrifying implications, but there passed through my mind the vision of Mella preparing supper, while her little boy sat in a chair turning the pages of a book ... It might have been one of my picture books, my aeroplane books, as Iris used to call them. I had no idea how old the child was; was he of an age to read? He was probably of an age to poke about and find what he wanted, even in the Augean Stables. I determined on the spot that I would never find out. About him or about anything else in Mella's life.

Heartened by this resolve, though I had no idea how I was going to implement it, I turned my Yale key in the lock. I stood still and sniffed the air. Margot's gloves were still on the ledge where they had been. The house seemed almost unnaturally quiet. Usually I left the wireless slightly on when I left home, and it welcomed me on my return. I turned the lights on and tiptoed towards the kitchen.

Everything looked different. There was a smell of something – could it be furniture polish? I hadn't known I had any.

In the electric light the whole house was strange and staring, like a cat's fur stroked the wrong way. I saw a piece of paper on the corner of the kitchen table, which had otherwise been stripped bare of books, papers, envelopes, breadcrumbs, ballpoints, old letters and picture postcards, including my mermaid. Then I remembered that I had torn the poor mermaid up. Had Mella noticed her absence?

Where had Mella put all these things? Apart from the note the table was ferociously empty.

So was the floor, I noticed. I seized the piece of paper, which was just a scrap torn off something. What would Mella say? 'Now that things are a bit cleaner I'll move in tomorrow. Yours, Mella.' But the note was in the form of a list. It puzzled me for a moment.

Ajax Fairy liquid mop wringing bucket dusters stiff brush.

It was Mella's shopping list. Things she needed for the house – my house. She must have forgotten to take it when she went away. And she might be back at any moment. I looked around me with a hunted feeling. At least she had no key. And she had her little boy to look after. She could hardly be back until tomorrow morning. But tomorrow morning she almost certainly would be back.

And so she was. I awaited her arrival in a fatalistic mood. At first I hardly knew she was there, because there was only a very faint scratching and tapping at the front door. The electric bell had been getting weaker for some reason, and now it hardly functioned at all. I had put a note outside the door for the postman and deliveries saying 'Please knock very hard – bell very weak' – but Mella was too tentative to obey this injunction.

And yet she came in briskly enough. I at once dreaded that brisk-ness; I knew what it portended. She was carrying a large plastic bag, from which the stiff brush protruded. She had not forgotten any of the items she had written on that list. The mop was there too.

'I must pay you for these,' I said faintly.

'If you like,' returned Mella, without interest; and she began at once on a floor that had not yet been 'done'.

I retreated into the front room, although I knew it would be only a temporary refuge. Mella had obviously been in here the day before, because efforts had been made to clear the floor and the top of the big Victorian desk which had once belonged to J.R.R. Tolkien, creator of *The Lord of the Rings*, at which Iris used to write her letters. It had been heaped up with books and papers of every description, lying there undisturbed for the last five years, since Iris had ceased to use it. She had no longer been able to manage any letter-writing. After her death I found innumerable sheets of paper which began 'Dear' or 'Darling', and got no further.

Mella had managed to find other homes for the books by piling them on top of the shelves, and she had arranged the mass of papers in orderly piles. An item at the top of one caught my eye. It was a number of white cards, which Mella had put neatly together. Each card had a Christian name written on it in Iris's firm, bold hand – John, Janet, Eric, Joanna, Angie ... They were Iris's '*placement*' cards.

In the old days, when we had a dinner party, Iris used to write each guest's name on a card and put it by their allotted place at the table. She took it seriously too, spending a lot of time working out the variations in the way guests could be deployed. She did this with calm concentration, while I was getting agitated over the stove or furiously chopping lettuce and tomatoes to make some sort of salad. It may have struck guests as incongruous that while the cutlery and plates were not exactly clean, and their wine glasses had a rather smeary appearance, so much loving care had none the less been exercised over their positions at the table, and the cards that directed them to it.

If there was a difficult guest present, Iris would always take that guest on herself, refusing to admit to me beforehand that any problem existed. Nor did it, thanks to her. Dinner parties always went well, certainly not by reason of the cooking, nor from the virtues of the wine, although there was always plenty of the stuff on the table. Seeming to negate the traditional concept of an accomplished hostess, Iris took care of the guests in her own way, making them relaxed and the evening a success.

When I saw the cards I felt suddenly angry that Mella had found them and stacked them up tidily like that. She had no business to do it! The feeling of a threat from her made me feel cross instead of just intimidated. I would speak sharply to her, tell her to leave things alone. What a nerve the girl had! Coming here and taking up the business of house-cleaning for me without being asked! I even found myself clenching my fists. If this went on I would have to show her what was what. *If* it went on? I would stop it at once! I would go back into the kitchen and tell her thank you very much but you can go now, and if you don't mind I don't want to see you again for the present.

For the present? Who was I kidding? The thought of a Mella-less future suddenly seemed curiously bleak. To that extent had she somehow climbed inside my life, my life as a widower. It put me in quite a panic to realise it.

But panic dulled into a sort of resignation, even apathy. I started idly to turn over the old cards – pretty grubby most of them – which Mella had stacked up. Those old dinner parties, before Iris became ill, seemed very far away. I remembered the animation and the pleasant intimacy of *tête-à-têtes*, eating bits of cheese, smoking Gauloises, drinking too much wine. How long ago it all seemed.

I was abruptly tugged from my reveries by a name on one of the cards. Margot! I looked for Guy but his name was not there. Had Iris taken the card away when Guy died? It seemed unlikely, but she might have done. Margot had come to us more often after that. Her name was still there.

Another thought – Mella had probably seen it? But it couldn't have meant anything to her? No possible reason to connect it with the driving gloves beside the front door. Mella couldn't possibly have started feeling jealous of all the female names she had found on the cards.

Then I remembered something else. The last letter I had got from Margot must have been lying on the kitchen table, amongst all the rest of the junk. Had Mella seen that, and read it? It was, so far as I could recall, a jolly, affectionate sort of letter, with nothing specifically embarrassing about it. To a stranger it could mean much or little. But it certainly mentioned that she was coming, and when.

Was that why Mella had appeared yesterday, and had seemed so conscious of another female presence in the house?

I became aware at this point that the sounds of banging and brushing, which had been so audible in the background, had now ceased. How still it was in this part of the house. I had noticed it before. It seemed even stiller now. I stood motionless, as alert as a hunted animal. I noticed I was still holding Iris's *placement* card, with 'Margot' on it, in my hand, and hastily put it back in the pile.

Then I called out, 'Mella, don't do too much, will you!' in what I hoped were placatory tones.

There was no reply. Could she have gone? Impossible, I would have heard her going. Besides, I realised, I didn't want her to go. I should have felt worried and unhappy, and there would have been a void, with nothing to do. I stole to the kitchen door and peered round it. Mella was sitting on a chair, with her hands hanging down on either side. Her eyes were closed. Her face was extremely pale.

Good heavens! Had the girl had a heart attack or a fit? Through my mind went the memorable words of Lady Macbeth when the news of Duncan's murder, which of course she knows all about, is brought. She makes the most unsuitable exclamation possible in the circumstances, but a very natural one. 'Woe, alas! What, in our house?'

No, not in my house! Mella could not be allowed to have a heart attack here! Besides, the girl was far too young for one. It was much more likely to happen to me.

To me – in my house? I put aside the thought. But Mella had no right to be ill here! My indignation was absurd, but it was as natural as Lady Macbeth's exclamation (to which Macduff makes the dry rejoinder: 'Too cruel anywhere').

Mella must have heard me. She opened her eyes and stood up, quite briskly.

'Are you all right, Mella?' I said, as solicitously as I could manage.

'Of course I'm all right.' Mella spoke in her new 'positive' voice, with a strong hint of impatience in it.

'But what happened?'

'Nothing happened. I sometimes feel a bit faint, that's all. It passes quite quickly. I've done it since I was a child. It's nothing, really.'

'But can I bring you anything? A glass of water? Milk, or something?'

'No, no, I'm quite all right. What I'll do is just lie down a little. D'you mind if I go upstairs?'

I suspected that Mella knew all about upstairs. She'd had plenty of time to find out yesterday.

'Of course not.'

'I can find my way, I'll be better quite soon, I promise.'

She promised. I felt rather touched by that, and by the way she said it. And I'd thought I'd never be touched or interested by anything that

Mella said or did. Well, now she had 'promised' and had proved me wrong.

I wondered what to do. The bed which Margot and I had slept in had been untouched after we got up. I wondered if she'd remembered to take her night-dress away or if she'd forgotten it, like the gloves. Margot had always had a habit of leaving things behind.

Parts of the floor were still wet from Mella's ministrations. There was a bucket of water on the floor, and the new mop was propped against the fridge. When Mella had arrived this morning with her plastic bag of cleaning substances, she had been carrying the mop like a spear.

I went quietly up the stairs. They, too, had been brushed and cleaned, I noticed. I supposed, not very hopefully, that Mella might be lying down in the little spare room where Margot had slept, at least where she had slept for most of the time. That too would bear ample traces of her occupation. A good thing if it did.

On my bed – our bed? *My* bed – Mella was lying flat on her back, her arms spread out as they had been in the chair downstairs. Her eyes were again closed and I could see no sign of breathing. I approached the bed, fascinated.

Mella sprang up, threw her arms round my neck and gave me several kisses at random. She continued to hug me, and I did my best to detach myself. She pulled me down beside her on the bed.

At least we were both fully clothed.

*

A couple of hours later we were not. Quite how this had come about was still uncertain to me.

After what had seemed a suitable lapse of time I had got up from beside Mella, asking how she felt now and making some remark, pleasant I hoped, about our having something to eat. Mella, after all, had never eaten in the house before. I had a vague hope that if she partook of bread and salt, as it were, in the way that Margot had, she might be propitiated, and feel herself to be on more or less even terms with that as yet unknown female presence.

But that was not how things turned out. Mella had jumped up when I moved and detained me by force. She was extremely strong, too. Suddenly she released me and said, 'I'm going to the bathroom. I won't be a minute.'

It was an extremely long minute. It was more like twenty minutes. I contemplated getting out of the house, or at least out of the bedroom. It was ridiculous to have been manhandled as I had been by a slip of a girl like Mella. But there, I was an old gentleman who had never been particularly strong at the best of times. None the less, I felt determined now, come what might, to stand my ground and stick up to Mella. Just like the hero of an old-fashioned school story, except that Mella, the school bully as it were, happened to be a girl. It would be a poor show, unsporting too, to run away. I would stand my ground, as much out of defiance of Mella, even resentment of her, as out of acquiescence in what she presumably had in mind.

She came back eventually, and of course she came back with nothing on. Her body was scrawny and unattractive, and it was somehow not a very nice colour either – no pink or white about it. But once more I felt touched, as when she had said in her suddenly shy confiding way, 'I promise'. There was a kind of mystery about her too, as she came, timidly now, across the room. I suppose there is about all women who unexpectedly appear naked, although there was nothing exactly unexpected about Mella's absence of clothes. She had, in a sense, given me plenty of warning.

She came up and kissed me, and then got straight into bed and pulled the duvet up over her head. It was obvious what I had to do, nor, on the whole, did I mind doing it. It was handing the situation over to Mella of course, rather as an admiral in the days of sail used sometimes to allow his opponent 'the weather gauge' in order to gain some other advantage than having the wind in his favour. I forget what the advantages were in the admiral's case, but in mine they seemed clear enough. If my relations with Mella were on this footing she would cease to persecute me with mops and brushes. Honour would be satisfied, and the house-cleaning need go no further. It seemed a crude bargain, but that was the way I saw it.

I thought about Iris. She did not seem so very far off now; not so far off as the dinner parties of those distant days. And she seemed to be smiling at me in her old way. I could almost hear her saying our old private recognition sign. 'Nom Nom.' And I loved hearing her say it. I felt she was agreeing that I had made the correct move.

*

The day was not yet over – far from it. I was feeling extremely hungry, and with a sudden movement I got out of bed before Mella could stop me. If, indeed, she had had a mind to do so.

It has often struck me that the worst thing about love is the business of getting dressed and undressed. Undressing had been quite easy because Mella's head had been well under the duvet, and her eyes presumably closed. But putting on my odd assortment of raggedy vests, my socks and my support stocking, under Mella's calm and – it has to be said – now placidly affectionate scrutiny, was quite an ordeal. I could feel her deciding to do something about my underwear, and as for my socks – well, I really ought to have washed them myself, some time ago.

Murmuring words to her about getting us something to eat I went slowly downstairs, pulling on my jersey. At that moment there came a robust knocking on the door, very different from the scratching sounds that Mella had produced that morning. I stopped in dismay. Whatever it was, probably nothing worse than the gas man or a charity or the local neighbourhood magazine, it came at an inconvenient moment. But I had better get it over with. I went to the front door.

It was Margot.

'Hullo, Johnny,' she said, walking straight in. 'I thought when I left you I'd call on Peggy and Mike, over at Kingston Bagpuize you know, and they persuaded me to stay the night. Look here, did I leave my gloves? Ah, thank goodness, there they are,' and Margot scooped them up in mid-sentence. 'I won't keep you,' she said. 'I expect you're busy.'

'Look here' was a favourite locution of Margot's. In someone else – a man with a moustache say – the old-fashioned turn of speech might have sounded a little abrupt, even hectoring. But with Margot it just sounded jolly.

I gazed at her with stupefaction. Somehow this classic situation, staple of so many French farces, was completely unexpected, wholly out of place in a widower's house, and its setting.

I had no leisure to reflect on this fact. Mella must have approached very quietly round the corner at the bottom of the stairs. Seeing Margot's face I turned quickly round and there Mella was, wearing my old dressing-gown which had obviously been just put on. Mella was still trying to tie the cord round herself.

I have never seen anyone look more delighted than Margot did at that moment. Sheer spontaneous joy shone on her face and sparkled in her eyes. I thought she was going to burst out giggling. And in fact, she was overcome by laughter as she seized both of Mella's hands.

'Hullo, my dear, *hullo*, my dear,' she chortled. 'I'm so glad to meet you! And what's your name?'

She said this exactly as she might have asked the same question of a little girl in a school. Mella didn't seem to mind in the least. In fact she looked almost as delighted as Margot. Her little face was wreathed in smiles, and she played rather provocatively with the cord of my old school-type dressing-gown.

Seeing them both look so delighted with the situation and with each other was, very naturally, a great relief to me. I saw at once that Mella must have heard Margot's voice, and known at once who it was likely to be. She may have come down with the intention of wiping her rival's eye: but the sight of Margot, and her face, must have removed any such impulse forthwith.

All the same, it was scarcely puzzling that Mella should have looked so pleased with the situation; and indeed with herself. In a sense it did her credit. Here she was, ensconced as it were, at the heart of what she must have thought of as Margot's territory; and her rival, so far from being cross, was being so charmingly gracious about it. In fact their response did credit to both of them.

Both women were now ignoring me completely. Mella was already telling Margot about her little boy, and her work, and her thesis, and all the difficulties she suffered under.

I looked at my watch. It was half-past three. Margot must have had lunch with Peggy and Mike, whoever they were, and come to me on the way home. I myself was hungrier than ever. I didn't bother to consider whether Mella was hungry or not. I felt that the two women had taken their affairs off my hands. And that was a relief. My own requirements I could look after myself. We drifted into the kitchen, with Mella and Margot still talking away nineteen to the dozen. They were a mother and daughter, reunited after a long and eventful separation. I was neither the father nor the son. Nor a husband either. I was just an old widower whose house had been taken over on behalf of a newly-formed, younger, more dynamic relationship, a sisterhood.

*

That was certainly what the situation began to look like. Where Mella was concerned I welcomed what I hoped would be a return to our previous placid and comparatively undemanding relationship, with its regular conversations and routines. Mella had found a new focus of interest, a new object in her life. It was ironic that this should be my old friend Margot, whom for only one exhausting day – exhausting for me that is – Mella had clearly regarded as a threat and a rival. For the first time it occurred to me how good Iris would have been with Mella; how much Iris would have helped her with whatever invisible and indefinable furies she felt herself to be pursued by.

But there was no point in my having that realisation now. Maybe Margot, who was still so very much alive and dedicated to whatever goal of the moment she could triumphantly score, would be able to sort out Mella's problems for her.

But if I supposed that I could now return to my old, simple, though undeniable need for Mella's company, and on the old terms, I was in for a rude awakening. True, she soon abandoned her house-cleaning activities, not with the uncompromising insouciance displayed by Margot, but enough to show that her heart and her emotions were no longer in it. Where were they then? I very sincerely hoped they might be with Margot, provided that left for me my former Mella, the old sleep-walking waif who had drifted to my door once or twice a week; who had been, I now recognised, so soothing to get on with, and so easy to entertain.

John Sparrow, the Warden of All Souls College, who had always been a cynophobe, if that is the correct term for a sincere detester of dogs, had once encountered at a tea party a quiet lady with a small dog, so very subdued that it was virtually unnoticeable.

'Your dog is almost as good as no dog at all, Madam,' he told her approvingly as he said goodbye.

I don't know whether the lady grasped how rare a compliment she and her dog had been paid; but the philosopher in Iris was amused by the notion, and it became one of our own useful categories. Children ('No man can be wholly bad if he hates dogs and children'), restaurants, students, parties, even marriages like our own – all could find an occasional place in the area of response suggested by Sparrow; and indeed already implicit in W.C. Fields' use of the original Oscar Wilde joke. ('A man must have a heart of stone not to laugh at the death of Little Nell.')

In any case, Mella's visits, and Mella as a visitor, had been for me almost as good as no visit and no visitor at all. Which is not to say that I would not have seriously missed them had they been discontinued. Where would Sparrow and Fields have been, after all, in a world in which there were no dogs to dislike, and no children?

The meeting with Margot that morning had for some reason made me feel that I ought really to make further enquiries about Mella's little boy. She had once told me his name: at least she had once told me that she sometimes called him Damian and sometimes Darren; he liked both these names and so did she. To me they seemed a good deal worse than no name at all, but that was Mella's affair. At the time, it struck me as just another of those inexplicable things about Mella

which one took for granted. Besides, when Mella's personality had
abruptly become so alarming, projecting itself into mops and brushes
and house-cleaning gear, I had sworn in silent retaliation to find out
nothing else from her ever again, and never to ask another question.

*

Margot drove off home in her rescued gloves; Mella disappeared to
wherever Damian (or Darren) and Alison (or Angela?) awaited her.

But next day Mella was back, and at the same disconcerting hour
of ten in the morning. I was sitting in one of the two office chairs in
the kitchen, and she promptly took the other one. Lips parted and her
voice hushed as if with religious awe, she began to ask me questions
about Margot. Where had I met her? Where did she live?

Her interest surprised me a little. I had supposed that all such
matters must have revealed themselves during those torrents of intimacy in which the two women had indulged yesterday; but I now saw
that Margot had probably heard everything about Mella, but that
Mella was by no means in the same position with regard to Margot.
To my dismay the temperature of intensity appeared to be rising. I
made an offer of Nescafé and the biscuit, but it was ignored. Instead
Mella pulled herself closer to me, the oversized castors of the office
chair rumbling over the wooden floor like the gun-trucks of a man-
of-war. 'Showing her teeth', I remembered, was the phrase used of a
warship running out its guns. I hoped Mella was not going to show
hers.

'John, I don't want to upset you. You've been through such a bad
time ... I know, because ...'

Although I had invited Mella long ago to call me John, she had only
used the name very rarely and tentatively, as if she feared to be taking
a liberty.

'You're going through one too?' I supplied helpfully.

Mella looked rather annoyed at that. Her speech this morning was
full of those moments which writers indicate by three dots ... Her eyes

now had a faraway look, as if she were pining for Margot in distant Norfolk.

'It's worse in the night of course,' she said.

This last observation seriously alarmed me. Margot was safely away in distant Norfolk, but if Mella took to proposing nocturnal visits to me the circuit would be closed. My house, I felt wildly, would no longer be mine, but hers as well. And what about Damian/Darren and the obliging Alison/Angela? No doubt they would be quite happy together if Mella took to spending nights with me. I was in something very near panic. Perhaps Mella saw this: perhaps she misunderstood it.

'*I* know what it's like,' she emphasised again, in an unexpectedly high, crowing voice. The castors rumbled; the chair, like an eighteen-pounder on the gun-deck, moved even closer to me, and Mella seized my hand in a grip which, as I knew from yesterday, was something very like iron. She drew my own chair towards herself, and now we seemed more like a pair of invalids in a nursing home, beginning what might become, if things prospered, a passionate relationship.

One thing led to another but, thank goodness, our relationship showed no signs of being like that. We went to bed, certainly, as we had done the day before; but I think it was probably just because we had done it the day before that we now must have felt something like a mutual obligation to do it again. Politeness, really. Each felt the other must be expecting it.

Mella was usually a reliable conversationalist, but she seemed to believe in silence in bed, as if she were in church, and if I ventured some more or less light-hearted comment her reply took a physical form, accompanied by some heavy breathing. Yet carried away by passion we certainly were not, although Mella's nakedness continued for me to have something unexpectedly and mysteriously touching about it.

Soon it became a ritual like our other routines; the Nescafé, the biscuit, and our always relaxed and undemanding talk. We added yet another routine: a short walk round the block after we got out of bed.

This was almost the same walk that I used to take many times a day with Iris, when she was ill.

*

I had heard nothing from Margot, and disliking the telephone as I did, I never attempted to ring her. Relations with Mella seemed to have settled down quite comfortably. And yet I always felt a slight reluctance, when she turned up, usually at ten in the morning or half-past, to engage in the first and most strenuous part of our routines of meeting. It was not a good time of the day to be going back to bed. I sometimes felt tempted to beg off it, but I could not see how that could be done without causing offence.

There was nothing to be done about it, any more than there was when, as a child in London, I used to be taken by my mother to a weekly gymnasium class, somewhere near the back of Sloane Square Underground station. My weekly apprehensions about this were greatly enhanced by my fear of the station itself, at which we arrived by train after the short journey from Gloucester Road. I loved the Underground and its stations, but I dreaded arriving at Sloane Square which, no doubt because of its proximity to the gymnasium, always struck me as an evil and sinister place, inhabited by hirsute ogres and fairies with bad taste, for the passages leading to the exit were in those days rough brickwork, slapped over with paint of a peculiarly sickly green.

By the time we got to the gym I would be feeling thoroughly depressed, nor were my fears allayed by the sight of Mr Macpherson and his cherubic assistant. But they were friendly enough; and by the time the hour was over I had quite enjoyed the gym class, just as, about sixty-five years later, I found myself quite enjoying my encounters in bed with Mella.

Mella seemed to like them too, but one could never be quite sure; indeed with her one could never be quite sure of anything. I sometimes had the feeling that we were both engaged in what Iris and I used to call a 'Gore'. Some friend had told us about a Mr Gore who had isolated a particular social situation, and named it after himself. It occurred when he was staying with a friend. This friend had suggested visiting a church. Mr Gore had no great wish to see this church, and neither, as he intuited, had his friend; but politeness required a show of enthusiasm on both sides, and, after all, the period of the visit had to be got through somehow ... With Mella I felt that our love-making rather resembled a 'Gore'. Neither of us were all that keen, but neither of us liked to say so. And it was as good a way as any of passing the time.

Iris and I were partial to terms and phrases like the 'Gore'. Another one we used was 'barnacling'. The great whales, as I had read some-where, lesser cetaceans too, as well as huge fishes like the whale shark (memorably encountered by Thor Heyerdahl during the voyage of the Kon-Tiki) have the habit of rubbing off the barnacles on their backs against some convenient large object: a ship, a pier, even another whale.

The analogy explains itself, and yet I was in two minds about it. Did I want to rub Mella off against Margot? Did I at least want to attempt it? The widower part of me, the part that wanted a quiet life and no further trouble, was certainly attracted by the idea. But did I really want to lose Mella, despite the rather more exacting form which her society had recently been taking?

After my first reaction, which had been one of relief, I had begun to feel rather less than pleased by Margot's unalloyed delight in the relation between Mella and myself, on which she had so unexpectedly stumbled. A little resentment – even a touch of jealousy – would surely not have been out of place? Margot's fascination with the newcomer, as apparently revealed in the sheer ebullience of that meeting, had seemed to reveal uncompromisingly that her fondness for myself had no trace of possessiveness about it.

Of course no widower wants his close friends to be tiresomely possessive. That went without saying. But equally no widower wants to feel that he is a bit of a burden, whom his friends would be thankful to transfer to other shoulders, if a willing pair of these happened to present themselves.

All of us, and not just widowers, might wish on occasion to barnacle an inconvenient friend. But to be barnacled oneself is quite another matter.

*

The barnacling business was in its nature a kind of comedy. But I was not inclined to find anything comic in the letter I received from Margot a few weeks later.

My Darling Johnny,

(Not having yet read the letter I was touched by the 'My Darling', although I could have done without the Johnny.)

You'll never guess what's been happening here! Wot larks! On Wednesday your Mella turned up out of the blue! When I saw you together I thought she was a nice little thing, and I was so pleased for you both. You *needed* something like that, you know. I still think she's nice – in fact I'm becoming very fond of her – but what a business, good heavens! I can't help wondering if you had any idea!

To begin with, of course, the girl is a consummate liar. But one can't blame her a bit. It's so pathetic, and her story is so sad. I don't suppose you've heard it, except for the special items she wanted to make you believe. No little boy of course, as she told you, and indeed as she told me when I called in at your place to pick up my gloves. All that came out when she'd been crying on my bosom for about two hours, after she showed up here. She really is a waif and stray, you know. I expect she wanted you to feel that there was nothing for you to worry about – that she had not only her child but a great friend, even an ex-husband, was it? – supporting her in the background. So you wouldn't have to feel you need do anything.

Well, that all disappeared with me of course. No child, no

husband, no girlfriend. Did she ever tell you how and where she had been living? Probably not. A wretched half a room over a shop run by some Indians, and they made her pay thirty quid a week. She wouldn't have wanted to let you know about that – you might have thought you ought to help her with money – and so she invented the child and the girlfriend. To reassure you I really think. She's not a natural liar. By nature, I think, she's as honest as the day. But what a time she's had! And no one, absolutely no one, in the University of Oxford to give her a helping hand. She's quite alone in the world.

She can stay here with me of course as long as she likes, and I really think that's the best thing. Oxford's no good to her, although she's a brainy little thing too, and there was some work she was doing for you wasn't there? Best forgotten about, I should think – for the moment anyway. What she needs is a complete rest. I can give her that here. Peace and quiet, and proper food at last. I gather she didn't even like to ask you for anything to eat when she came to see you!

Well, no point in going on. I'll keep you in touch with her if you like, although I really think it's best for her to be quite on her own for a while – and that she can be here with me. She's a dear creature. As I said, I'm getting very fond of her.

Now look after yourself. I don't think you feed yourself properly, so of course you couldn't be expected to do Mella.

So much love to you XXX
Margot

I read the whole letter, and then I read it again. As I finished it, I decided that the subtlest insult in the whole thing was the sting in the tail. Margot wouldn't have known it was an insult of course, or have used the word in any way deliberately. She wouldn't have thought that anything in her letter was at all insulting. Why should it be? The facts about poor Mella and her travails spoke for themselves. Nobody's fault. Except, of course, for the villainous Indian grocer, who was charging her thirty quid a week. If he really was.

Why couldn't Margot have written at the end, 'So of course you couldn't be expected to *feed* Mella?' More natural surely? Whatever the wounding implications of that too might be. But no, through some quirk of her own Margot had preferred to write that I 'couldn't be expected to *do* Mella.' It sounded as if sex-wise, too, the poor old gentleman was obviously not up to it, just as he couldn't be expected to care for Mella; to cherish her problems; to cope with her and, if need be, to control her. Even to find out anything about her.

As I pondered all that I began to laugh. Margot's letter was comic, after all. And the odd verb she had made use of at the end was probably fully justified. I just couldn't 'do' Mella in any sense. As Margot obviously could.

When Mella's daily visits stopped I had been rather relieved. I hoped we might have reverted, with some minor differences, to our previous undemanding itinerary, on a weekly or fortnightly basis. I hoped so. But I had missed her. And of course I couldn't stop thinking about her.

I was genuinely surprised to hear that she had no child. The very fact that she had not talked about her little boy, knowing that I would not be interested, had always seemed to me – now that I came to think about it – an implicit proof of the child's existence. Because I knew no more of little Damian, or little Darren, than the name, it had never occurred to me to doubt that he must be running about somewhere, attended, when she could manage it, by the faithful Alison, or Angela.

There was no reason either why Mella should have told me of the grocer problem. She had never given the slightest sign of being short of money. Of course I should have asked her; and yet why should I? She had a college where someone was responsible for her. She must have had enough money to continue with her studies, taking her own time. I wasn't even her supervisor. I had just been asked to see her a few times on topics in which she was said to be especially interested; and I had certainly done that. In fact I had been seeing her once or twice a week now for at least a year. Longer.

And yet Margot was right. Of course she was right. I had never wanted to find out about Mella, or to help her, come to that. I had just gone along with what she seemed to want; and it looked now as if she had hardly known herself what she did want. Except, when the chance offered, to flee to someone like Margot, to weep on her bosom, to confess and confide her troubles, to be fed and comforted, to stay as long as she wanted ...

Well, I had at least done that for Mella, however accidentally. I had put her in touch with the right person; and she, leaping out of my bed, had shown the initiative to do the rest.

And now I was missing her. I was very much missing her. Nor did there seem to be any prospect of seeing her for a long time. Comfortably settled with Margot in Norfolk (and how had she got there? Train or bus, I supposed) there seemed no reason why she should ever leave. I paused to consider Margot's own motives in the matter. I brushed aside the vulgar idea that she might be a bit lesbian. And so might Mella herself, come to that. But to suppose such a thing was a typically glib masculine reaction to the natural kindness of women to other women? Their fellow-feeling, their desire to rush in and rescue a lame duck. Iris herself had been always prepared to help and counsel and comfort, although naturally she couldn't provide the amenities, in the way of house and hospitality, which Margot could easily manage.

All the same, there might be some possibility that Margot had a *tendresse* at times for persons of her own sex. Or that Mella had. Why not? Perhaps Margot had fallen in love with her? Or each with the other? What seemed certain was that I should not be seeing Mella for a long time. If at all. The thought caused me annoyance rather than sadness. I should miss the simplicity of our relationship, the undemandingness. Taking each other for granted ...

For Mella Margot's arrival had perhaps been a turning-point? The big chance in life, an offer of salvation? Who could say? They would certainly not be taking each other for granted.

Another annoying thing was that the invisible presence of Margot had clearly galvanised Mella into going to bed with me. I doubted that she would have wanted to do it otherwise. Nor would I. The idea had never occurred to me before. And if it had done so, I would have rejected it as quite unsuitable. Mella was not exactly my pupil, but our relationship was still a formalised one: that of student and teacher. It was entirely because of Margot, the outsider, that a sudden change had been precipitated.

And Margot and I had neither made love nor, so far as I could remember, had we intended to do so. Just one, or two, of life's little ironies, as poet and novelist Thomas Hardy would say. I loved almost all Hardy's books; but I didn't greatly care for the way he overworked his little ironies.

CHAPTER FOUR

The Falling Snow

All these things being so, what happened next was the last thing I expected. But that was how it was, anyway. Mella appeared at the door at ten o'clock the next morning.

It was early December now. Iris had died at the beginning of the previous February. Another winter was well under way. The weather had suddenly changed and gone very cold. In the night it had started to snow, and though there was very little left on the ground, small, damp flakes were still falling. In the snow light Mella looked more than ever insubstantial and waif-like. I gaped at her.

'Mella! I thought you were with Margot!'

She stumbled across the doorstep like the orphan of the storm who has come home at last to a safe place to die. I retreated before her. In a second we were in the kitchen, and Mella was seated on one of the office chairs.

'Nescafé? Your biscuit?'

Mella smiled wanly. She said nothing. I put the kettle on for the coffee and opened the biscuit tin. As I turned to fill her mug, Mella was suddenly on me. Her arms went tightly round my neck. The mug which I had been about to fill went flying across the room. Mella's face was against my nose. I had difficulty in breathing. I wondered with some annoyance if the mug was broken – I was rather fond of that mug – and I made efforts to wriggle out of Mella's grasp.

'Please, John,' she was saying. 'Let me come to you. I'll look after you, I promise. I won't bother you. I'll go out. I'll clean the house and everything.'

If she hadn't mentioned the house, and cleaning it, she would have had a better case. That was a caddish thing to think, but I did think it.

The idea of the house, my house, a house which had been cleaned by Mella, was instantly and totally insupportable.

'But what about your little boy?'

'All right, I don't have a little boy. I made that up. And about my husband. Why shouldn't I? I thought that if I said about those things you wouldn't be worrying about me.'

I wouldn't be worrying about her, as a woman on her own. So it was all done for my sake, really. That might have been touching. Perhaps it was intended to be. But I failed to be touched. She was studying my face, or at least looking at it closely. It must have looked full of dismay, guilt, embarrassment: all sorts of things like that. But chiefly my face felt as if it belonged to a small boy at school, who has been made some outrageous proposition by a school chum – climbing the chapel roof, pinching the master's gown – and who doesn't know how to get out of it without losing too much face.

In the midst of these horrors a thought struck me. Mella had made up the child, the husband and so forth, just as Margot had written. But how much else might she have made up? Margot had contradicted herself. She had said Mella was a consummate liar, but also that she was not a natural liar, and was as honest as the day.

Maybe she was. I was not exactly a gem of truthfulness myself. I had certainly been taken in about the child, but I began to wonder now about some of the other things Mella had 'confessed' to Margot. Was it a question of owning up to one lie, and after that everyone will start believing you?

I said boldly: 'I'm worried now about how you live, darling, and where you live. I don't think it would be a good idea being here, but what about your digs? Can't we get you better ones? Can I help?'

I put the darling in a bit self-consciously. I had never called her darling before. When I was together with Mella, as I now realised more and more, we had our own thing, our own way, of being ourselves. We were not in darling circles. I was glad we weren't, but none the less I had made a mistake, a fatal mistake. Mella's eyes narrowed, and her lips compressed. I felt like the captain of a seventy-four who has unavoidably allowed his opponent to cross his stern, so that he is about to receive the blast of a thirty-seven gun broadside.

'For what we are about to receive ...' was supposed to have been the chant on deck in the terrible slow seconds before the enemy ship opened fire.

But Mella, gazing at me with a frightening air of devotion (I don't suppose the captains of rival ships ever did that), merely said, 'Where do you think I live, then?'

This was it. Devoted she might look, but there was a faint air of amusement too on Mella's face as she awaited my reply.

'I seem to remember you once mentioned the little shop you lived over? Handy in a way, I suppose.'

How could I have thought that was going to work? I was making one bloomer after another. Mella's mild little face now looked stern, like Portia's in the seat of judgement.

'Of course I never told you anything of the sort. You've been talking on the phone to Margot, haven't you? That skunk. That female bastard. She's been telling you all sorts of rotten things about me, hasn't she?'

'No, no,' I protested in alarm. 'I haven't spoken to her. She just wrote.'

Too late again, I realised my mistake. Mella had risen to her feet and was glaring down at me.

'Show me. Show me what she wrote.'

'No. I can't do that, Mella,' I said, with a feeble attempt at dignity.

Quite out of the question of course. But then I suddenly thought: why not? Margot had, after all, been so nice about Mella in the letter. I wouldn't mind reading those things about myself; indeed I would rather enjoy it. And to read about oneself in a letter is always, surely, irresistibly interesting. If I tried to keep the letter back, Mella would only grow more and more angry. And it was no use denying that I felt frightened of her now, when she showed signs of getting angry. Just as I had once found in my solitary state, that I could be a little frightened of Margot.

So I gave her the letter. Unable to bear looking at her while she read it, I picked up the broken mug and busied myself with making a fresh cup of coffee. Then I darted a fearful glance sideways at Mella's face. It was very pale. I thought she might be going to faint again. And apart from the pallor the face looked old. As old as Margot's. Almost as old as mine. How old was this girl, anyway?

I gave her the cup of coffee and she started to drink it without expression. I handed her the biscuit. That gave me a twinge too. I had handed Mella so many biscuits in our time. A nice simple heart-warming thing to do – giving people biscuits. People with whom one had a special relationship.

Too late, as usual, I knew that my real reason for showing Mella the letter, apart from sheer funk about how she might carry on, was to induce her to realise what a happy home she had presumably left in Norfolk; how sensible it would be to go back there to all the warmth and interest of Margot's hospitality.

Had she already quarrelled with Margot? Had they had a 'blood row', as it was called? But I couldn't believe it. Margot was kind, good-natured, easy-going. She loved to chatter away. And Mella talked enough when she was with me, for God's sake. I could see she might, on getting to know her at home, have felt a bit inhibited with Margot and her style of action, but surely she would get over that very soon. What could have gone wrong? I asked the question directly. Mella promptly dissolved in tears.

'How could you have read that letter she sent you,' she blubbered. 'How *could* you, how *could* you? I didn't want you to know that I was going, that I was there. Of course I didn't! It's ruined everything … It'll never be the same again, never.'

She had just been crying before, but now her face seemed to dissolve itself, like a baby's, into a single contortion of misery. I tried to put my arm round her shoulder. I even tried to kiss her. I had no experience of what to do in cases of such extreme emotion, of which I took this to be one. My Iris had never done anything of this kind. With other people perhaps, at some earlier stage of her life, but never with me.

In some strange way, Mella seemed to realise all this. She straightened up and blew her nose.

'Sorry,' she said coldly.

'That's all right.'

It was borne in upon me somehow that they hadn't had a quarrel at all. Being over there with Margot had somehow given Mella the nerve and the resolution to come back straight to Oxford, and make me the proposition that she had just made. And the whole thing had been ruined, as she may have seen it, by that letter I had received from Margot. Why on earth had I been such a fool as to show it to her, and to let her know that I had heard about her from Margot? But really, I knew I was glad that I had shown it. And suffered the consequences: which is another way of saying that I had escaped them.

Outside, I noticed, the small flakes of wet snow were still falling. It looked thoroughly miserable. Not a day to travel on. Not a day to do anything but keep snug and warm at home. In one's house. My widower's house.

But, on the other hand, it was not a day on which to be by oneself either. Much better, if one could, to be at home with somebody else? I looked at Mella. Mella looked at me. I said nothing. Then she got up and adjusted herself and took her bag. She was never without that.

'Shall you go back to Norfolk now?' I quavered.

She did not reply. I dithered after her to the front door. She opened it herself and turned back for a moment.

'I *hate* Margot.'

She ran through the snow to the garden gate, turned the corner and disappeared.

I stood gazing stupidly at the falling snow. But only for a few moments. Then I ran back to the kitchen, got my cap and coat, and followed her out into the garden. If she had disappeared I might have run after her, tried to find her. But there she still was, a small figure, trudging up the straight street in the snow. I had an impulse to shout after her, but I didn't. I gazed until she was lost to sight round a corner and then went back into my house and shut the door.

*

I wrote to Margot, but there did not seem much to say, for I was disinclined to tell her what had really taken place. The worst of the trouble seemed to have been caused by my own stupidity, if it was no worse than that, in letting Mella know that I had heard from Margot, and then letting her see the letter. It was obvious to me now why I had done this. A few days with Margot had been enough to make Mella decide to come back to Oxford, and to move in on me and my house. For that was what it came to. It was even possible that Margot had encouraged her to try taking this course. In spite of what she had written, Margot had no doubt had enough of Mella's company after not many days.

It was also possible, it was even likely, that the two had held a council of war, at which Margot had urged bold measures on the younger woman. Nothing venture, nothing win. I shrank from the odious complacency entailed on me by that supposition. It was hateful to see oneself as pursued by designing women; but more hateful still to envisage the determined selfishness with which one would plan counter-moves, measures with which to fight them off.

And I knew quite well that it was not only hateful, it was also misleading. Only in silly plays and soap operas, or novels like Mrs Gaskell's *Cranford*, do plots to inveigle men into marriage get hatched. They are a literary device, not a true reflection of human nature. Human nature deals in impulses, often conflicting or irrational, which besiege the consciousness, storming and abandoning it again from day to day. One never knows what it might do, or feel, next.

Why had Margot come to my bed in the night? Why had Mella become so different so suddenly when she knew that another woman had been in the house? Surely no deep strategy was involved in these actions; they were just a part of human behaviour, its diversions as one might say, bringing about both troubles and rewards.

Well, it was all very well to say that, and even to feel it. Was I myself a good example of this Law of Impulsive Behaviour? I might think not, when I considered how selfish I was about my house and about the kind of life I thought I wanted to live in it. And yet, just think of the dangers to that way of life which I seemed to have been deliberately letting myself in for lately!

I could easily have got in a real mess with Mella. Not marrying her of course, nothing so antique as that, but sharing my house with her. For not only did I feel sorry for her, at least by fits and starts, but I also wanted her company. I needed it, on my own terms of course; but until lately Mella had always seemed perfectly happy to accept those terms. Assuming, of course, that she was aware of them; and I myself was well aware that one could not always make such an assumption.

But why had I not run after her through the snow and asked her to come back to the house, to be there, if she wanted, for a day or two, so that we could begin to get to know each other? And all that. Which we hadn't done before. Because I had not wanted us to get to know each other?

*

Iris died a year ago.

I had wanted this to be an especially quiet time. It was not. And no doubt it's better that it should not have been. I think of the way she used to laugh as she quoted a song, or hymn, sung at school.

> Come, we must be up and doing,
> With a heart for any fate!

She always did have a heart. And perhaps one for any fate, too. I only wanted one kind of fate: being in my house and living to myself and for myself. Not much to ask? But other people seemed to think it was. Much too much. Look at all the trouble I'd lately been having. Did I want that trouble? I thought I didn't, but one could never be sure. People like trouble. I thought suddenly of Margot's face, looking over my shoulder on the doorstep, looking at Mella. Margot's large well-wishing features had been absolutely transformed. She might have been told she was going to give birth to the Saviour or something, instead of meeting the girl with whom I had just been in bed, the bed to which Margot herself had paid a nocturnal visit the night before. It had been *exciting* for Margot; it seemed to me to be as simple as that. And so, old as I was and set in my ways, like a hermit crab in its adopted shell, hadn't I better try to find ways myself of finding life exciting?

Suppose, for a start, that I said to Mella when I next saw her – she was bound to come back in a day or two – supposing I said: 'Mella, I'm really very fond of you, you know.' I would say it in firm tones, indicating exactly what I meant. 'I'm very fond of you.' I remembered from school, or from something I'd read, that there is a fatal French phrase, '*je t'aime bien*' – fatal because it reveals, with unforgiving French logic, the difference between saying 'I'm fond of you' and 'I love you' – '*je t'aime*'. The English try to soften the blow. The French will have none of that. They may not have many words, but they know how to use them incisively. '*Je t'aime bien*' *should* be able to mean 'I love you well – I love you even more than loving you.' But it doesn't. Because of the fatal *bien* it can only mean 'I like you a lot,' or, with the blow slightly softened, 'I'm really very fond of you.'

But what's the point of that? What it comes to is that I can't say to Mella: 'I love you.' Why not? There would be no harm in saying it, but I can't. I never said it to Iris – at least I don't think I did. There was no need to, and it never occurred to me. But I wouldn't say it to Mella, or to anyone else, on principle.

So it's principles now, is it? What about the Law of Impulsive Behaviour? If you can cheer the lady up by suddenly saying, 'I love you', why not do it? She may not believe you, but that's not the point. She'll be pleased, anyhow. Even comforted.

I should have run after Mella in the snow and said, 'I love you.' What would she have done? Turned around and trudged on? Alternatively, she might have flown like a bird into my arms (but I am seventy-four and slightly built) and said, 'I love you too.'

A fortnight later I was no longer interested in the question of whether or not to say 'I love you' to Mella. I just wanted to see her. I wanted to see her badly, and I was deeply upset and disturbed by her absence. If she returned I should not bother about 'I love you' … I should say ... What should I say? 'Come and try living in my house for a bit if you like.'

Mella did not reappear. And I got very low. I wondered whether she could possibly be back with Margot. I rang Margot. Margot sounded no longer very interested in Mella. She had a daughter there, with her children.

'Don't worry,' said Margot. 'I expect she'll turn up in a day or two.'

She did not. I meditated unhappily. I had spoilt her life. Perhaps she would end up as a drug addict or a prostitute? And it had been so pleasant to be together, in terms of a biscuit and a cup of Nescafé ... After a few more days I decided to ring her college. I still remembered which it was. After a bit of trouble I got through to the Tuition Secretary. She was a helpful woman, but she knew nothing about the whereabouts of Mella, who had long since ceased to have an official college connection.

'The lodge may know something about her,' she suggested.

I tried ringing the college lodge, but they were always busy, so I decided to walk down there. I was nervous of buses, and parking a car had become quite impossible. The lodge was full of students, but a young woman (what had happened to college porters?) who had been busy on the phone was free at last and looked at me enquiringly. I asked if they had seen Mella Handley lately.

'Mella's gone away, hasn't she, Mr Pratt?' asked the lady of some invisible colleague in the inner office.

Mr Pratt couldn't say.

'Well, there's nothing in the pigeon-hole for her,' said the lady porter. 'She used to come in for her mail.'

I started wondering who the people were who had once written to Mella. Had they given up writing? It was hard to imagine Mella as a correspondent. Had they not received replies?

I hung about in the quad, at a loss for what to do next. Then I saw the lady porter emerge with a bag and the satisfied air of one who has finished their tour of duty. She saw me too, and her features became friendly.

'Little Mella, wasn't it, you were asking for? We're sorry she's gone,' indicating her colleagues behind her in the lodge with a wave of the hand. 'We all liked her.'

'Where did she live, d'you know?' I asked.

The lady porter was obviously reluctant to return to the scene of her labours to find out the address, and I did not press the point.

'Oh, she had a lovely flat,' she said instead. 'It was up Parktown way. I used to visit there you see, because Mella loved my kids – two little boys they are – Damian and Darren. And she was that kind, I could leave them with her sometimes. Thought the world of her, the children did. Always giving them presents.'

'Did you meet her friends at all, a boyfriend perhaps? Someone told me she was married.'

'Oh no, she certainly wasn't married. Very much on her own, she was. I never saw any friends at her flat.'

I thanked the lady porter and we parted company. I remembered to ask if Mella had left any address behind her, for forwarding of mail. She had not done so.

'But,' said the lady, whom I now began to think of as my friend and ally, 'I've known her take herself off for a week or two, longer sometimes, and be back when I next gave her a call or dropped in with the boys. You never quite know where you are with Mella; but we've been so fond of her, you know. We'd miss her if she went for good, but I don't think she has done, not now. She'll be back again one of these days. Did you want to leave a message?'

I said no, thank you very much, and I thanked the lady porter profusely. It occurred to me that she should really be called the portress. Didn't Milton have such a person, on duty at Hell's Gate?

'We're here to help others, that's what I always say,' my own particular portress was going on in her comfortable manner.

I wondered if or how I could give her a tip, which would have been a commonplace in the old times of college porters. I decided that in our changed circumstances today it could only be inappropriate.

*

86

I can't say I missed Mella for long, or, indeed, Margot. I didn't in any case have to miss Margot because I went on seeing her from time to time. We sometimes talked about Mella; Margot asked if I missed her, and how important the relationship had been to me. I returned a vague reply because I didn't know myself. I had missed her; but what the lady porter had said about Mella had somehow deprived her in my eyes of the being she had possessed when she used to visit my widower's house, and have a mug of coffee and a biscuit. The things revealed by Margot's letter had also made a difference. Mella in bed, or Mella violently mopping the floor, had seemed perfectly normal extensions of the Mella who had come periodically scratching at the door. But after hearing about her flat, and her kindness to the lady porter's little boys (and they *were* called Damian and Darren) I found it hard to believe in Mella at all. Her disappearance seemed a natural thing, like that of someone seen on the tube, who gets out and walks away down the platform, leaving you thinking for a moment or two how nice it might have been to meet them.

CHAPTER FIVE

Limbo

The most unexpected aspect of bereavement, and the one hardest for a bereft person to identify, turned out, when I started thinking about it, to be the simplest of all. Everyone, even the very young, unconsciously grasps that daily life is founded on the principle of Sam and his brick wall; with age we become increasingly conscious of that principle, and learn to use it purposefully. Perhaps it's more a Law than a Principle. In any case, if you spend some time, like the proverbial Sam, banging your head against the wall, you know that the ensuing period, before the cycle starts up again, will be agreeable. Margot and Mella had made a fine wall to bang my head up against – Sam himself could have done no better.

In a more general way, bereavement, to my surprise, had at first removed the brick wall. By its nature bereavement entitled me to unlimited wall remission. Or so I supposed. I could concentrate on enjoying myself, my own life, my own time and routine. No wall appeared to be in the way. But that, it soon appeared, was just the trouble.

Walls have ears; they soon divined my intentions and set out to put things right. These obliging structures crowded on me from all sides, and when my head instinctively avoided them they peremptorily banged it for me.

What was I to do now without Margot looming up on one side, Mella on the other? I soon found out, for with Mella gone and Margot no longer so intent on suggesting a visit from me to her, or from her to me, I was thrown back on my own resources.

After the trouble I felt I had had with the two ladies, this should have been just what I wanted. A remission from the natural Law of

Sam and his wall. And indeed, it was very agreeable at first to live, as I thought of it, to myself and for myself. Agreeable to think about Margot and Mella, and to be grateful for their absence.

But after a few days I was not so sure. The two women and their – in some ways – equally vigorous personalities had given me willy-nilly a new personality of my own. A negative one no doubt, because evolved under stress for a special purpose. A personality specialising in self-protection.

Now I must try to develop into someone more like my old self, as I thought of it; a self more like the one who had been looking after Iris. I would wake up early and read or write in bed. I would walk regularly around the block, as I used to do with Iris. I would shop in a leisurely fashion. And all the time I would be looking forward to the evening, and the dark coming on; looking forward also, with the poor remains of an old pleasure, to my drink. Two drinks. More than that I knew by now to be a mistake. I would have a long vague supper over a book, with music on the radio. And maybe the TV a little later in the evening. I would cruise the five channels, each more idiotic than the last, and then switch it thankfully off, unless there happened to be a good car chase, some brisk shooting, a promising creature from outer space. I had really enjoyed such things once, and with Iris peacefully asleep upstairs they had all fitted cosily into the evening's routine. Now it was a relief to turn the box off and go to bed. With a pill.

*

Memory again began to take me over. Margot and Mella between them had distracted it, chopped it into pieces which lay writhing in the dust like severed dragons' heads; and at the time it seemed as if it would not grow again. But it was growing now, the pieces slithering swiftly together and reassembling themselves like those old, green, viscid beings from some horror movie who used to amuse and comfort me on the TV.

At first I welcomed the memories. Then I did not. But there was something at the back of my mind which came with them, and which seemed a familiar but invisible accompaniment. What was it? The thing irritated me because it seemed so real. Not like memory, whose reality was oppressive and overbearing, sweetly and insidiously compulsive, but without life.

Then it came back to me, and how could I have forgotten? It showed at least that my short-term memory was seriously impaired; so seriously that I at once began to wonder with apprehension whether that total recall of the last few months and years would, before I knew it, be gone the same way.

But at least I *had* remembered. Or rather it had come back to me. And what had come back was very simple: the fact that in those early mornings after Iris died, I had lain in bed and written about it all. (That was well before the arrival in my life of Margot and of Mella.)

Where had it gone, the stuff I had written? Had it gone to Pieland, to join the Original Great Pie, never refound? Mella's pies had replaced that legendary Pie, but now Mella's pies had themselves vanished. Into the limbo of things eaten or not eaten. Into the limbo of things equally lost, whether forgotten or recalled.

I began to search. I remembered Margot's apt reference to the Augean Stables. Mella's subsequent activities with pan and brush, mop and Ajax, had seemed dreadfully effective at the time, but time itself had gone on to mock them – scarcely a trace of those levellings and excavations now remained.

After opening and closing the same drawers and folders many times, and turning over the piles of old papers on the floor, as foxes turn cowpats over in pursuit of the beetles that lurk beneath, I gave it up. Why should I bother anyway? What I had scribbled down had given me something to do at the time, and might even have cheered me up, but that was all there was to it. I abandoned the search.

But a lingering curiosity remained. What sort of things had I put down then, and presumably thought it worthwhile to put down during that period of trance, when I seemed to live with the dead and not with the living? I had written things down. And I had agreed with what seemed now an almost pathetic relish to talk at a number of 'carers'' meetings and medical conferences, at which we had all seemed to be dementia sufferers, fans even, joined together in a fellowship of mutual comfort and interest.

I had a lot of letters from that time, which were still in a cardboard box on the kitchen table. I still received them, and still went quite often to the meetings, although Mella and Margot had made something of a temporary disruption. The letters were there, even though Pieland had claimed so many others, and I started idly to look through them. There was a dishevelled sheaf of paper underneath, twisted up athwart the bottom of the box.

I pulled a piece out, and instantly recognised what I had once written. It must have been less than a week after Iris died. It began quite abruptly; and I at once sat down to read it. I couldn't think at first what I had been talking about, but then it all began to make sense, of a kind. I was still amazed, as I read, by the way I had forgotten all about it, as if memory had lost all function and purpose now that Iris was dead, and could refer only to the time she had been ill, and we had been together.

*

During the night [so it began] I heard the voice of the lady at the supper table the evening before. 'Just beside him in the garden … such a suitable arrangement, don't you think? And they were both such keen gardeners …'

She was not talking to me but to her neighbour at the end of the table about some devoted couple, now deceased. As insomnia wore on and it began to get light I lay and pondered the advantages of the arrangement. I couldn't see any, I finally decided. Between listening to what my own neighbour was saying, and replying suitably, I tried to hear whether there had been any memorial to the couple. A small stone, as on a dog's grave, or perhaps just a patch of their favourite flowers? But if any detail had been given about this I had missed it.

I wished that I had sought out the woman in the drawing-room after dinner and gone into the matter thoroughly. But such a show of interest from one recently bereaved might not have seemed in the best of taste. My curiosity was natural, yet it could have been embarrassing for a fellow guest to satisfy. I had never met the woman before, and I scarcely knew the kind persons who had asked me to dinner.

I was well aware that they had thought I ought to be asked, to be 'brought out'. Brought out of whatever state of aloneness one should not be left in. But the couple buried in the garden, or rather under the garden, would not be alone.

That seemed to be the crucial point. They would have each other for company, as in life. What I was thinking about in the night, since I couldn't think of anything better to think about, was whether the friends supposed that the buried couple had enjoyed, before they died, the prospect of being together under the garden. Had they looked forward to it? Were they still enjoying it?

Perhaps it had been her idea, after he died, to put him in the garden. In which case had it been a surprise, and perhaps not an altogether welcome one, to find that his wife was being installed there beside him? By the time she arrived he might have settled down to the pleasures of being alone. And for some reason I liked the idea that he hadn't really been a keen gardener at all, but that in the interest of marital solidarity he had gone along with the version of himself that his wife had put about.

Endless possibilities. And all that really mattered was they had vanished from the world, into total existlessness. Speculation about their hypothetical feelings could none the less go on, in the same way that information could be exchanged about their physical where-abouts. There they were, in the garden; so must they in some sense not be aware of this comforting fact? It was certainly a comfort for others to suppose so.

The couple interred under the rosebed in their garden continued to exist in the consciousness of the living. In what Milton called the 'thoughts that wander through eternity'. And eternity is not in the afterlife but in our own minds. Communing with the dead in this way must be one of the oldest of all human indulgences. The Russian poet Tyutchev, a near contemporary of Pushkin, wrote a moving poem with the refrain: 'My Dear One, do you see me?' Better to be seen by one's dead wife than by God; but Tyutchev, a devout Orthodox believer, would be sure to have included the Deity along with his wife in this hope of living under perpetual observation.

To all this Thomas Hardy provides an illogical contrast. In Hardy's view of the matter God didn't actually exist, but He none the less contrived to keep Mr Hardy under close observation, just as Hardy's dead wife did, and his dog, and various other animals. True, Hardy only required their continued existence for the purpose of writing poems about them; but that, after all, is the best use a writer can possibly make of the dear departed – or of God himself, come to that. As poets who were able to make good use of their material, the devout believer Tyutchev and the wistful atheist Hardy are a long way from being far apart.

As I was lying in bed the next night, I started wondering about the obvious fact that people today who have no belief either in God or in an afterlife should none the less continue to feel that their loved ones are still there, still aware of their situation, whether reposing in the garden, or the churchyard, or as a handful of ashes in an urn. The dead expect the attentions the living bestow on them; and almost unconsciously the living assume that this must be so. Certainly a beliefless Hardy clung to the notion of, as it were, poetic survival. In his verses the dead continue to converse with the living, quarrel with them, patronise them for still being above ground, become satirical at their expense. They can be downright nasty sometimes too.

Well, and why not? Sometimes Hardy comes clean. In one poem 'a dead man's finer part' is kept alive in the hearts of those who loved him, like human tissue under a slide or in a bell jar, until the moment when memory and mortality fail, and one feeble spark is left in no other heart but that of the poet – where it is 'dying amid the dark'.

Writing about the dead is not only a way of continuing to feel in touch with them, but also of expiating guilt. As soon as his wife Emma died, Hardy visited the village in North Cornwall where he met her, and poured out a stream of the most wonderful poems about that first magical meeting time, alleging that he was just the same as when

Our days were a joy and our paths through flowers.

No wonder wife number two – Florence – used, privately and rather sourly, to refer to her predecessor as 'the late espoused saint'.

She had much to put up with, including the fact that although Hardy referred to himself, in one of his most haunting poems, as 'a man who used to notice such things', he turned the blindest possible eye to his own domestic situation, preferring not to notice how it functioned, and at what cost and what sacrifice to whom. In that respect, no doubt, he was not a unique and original poet, who saw the hedgehog in the warm and mothy summer darkness travelling 'furtively over the lawn', but a man who resembled – and outwardly at least preferred to resemble – all the many other deliberately unseeing men of his age.

Hardy's poetry flourished alike on his lack of belief and on his devotion to the uses of poetic survival. In one poem to the dead Emma he acknowledges her 'existlessness'. But when he came to revise the poem he substituted the phrase 'wan wistlessness'. A beautiful Hardy coinage, very Old-English in feeling. It should mean, literally, not being in a position to have thoughts or consciousness, although in Hardy's own poetic mind the dead Emma goes on having plenty of both. The phrase is wistful as well as wistless, but 'wan', which in Old English meant dark or gloomy, weakens the effect; for by Hardy's time it had become a washed-out little word, suitable for a state of non-awareness. 'Existlessness' is much better, more uncompromising, even though it is contradicted by everything else about the continued existence of Emma, in this poem and in many others.

It cheers one up, in a way, to brood about such matters. I see why Hardy wrote those poems about Emma immediately after his wife died. Not only was she still very much there for him, but she carried him back, as in 'After a Journey', to the days and the places where he first met her. To write about her made him feel just the same as when their 'days were a joy and their paths through flowers.'

With me the effect is the opposite. I can write about Iris again now, as I used to before she died ten days ago. But I am writing about her the other way round. Hardy kept Emma alive, at least for a while, by writing about her. I felt that Iris was alive with me until this morning. Now I feel, quite suddenly, that she really has ceased to exist, and that is why I must write about her as if she were still alive. I feel that she has gone. But there seems rather more to it than that. I *know* that she has gone. She was here yesterday, and the day before, and the day before that. But not now. This morning I went down to the kitchen at six o'clock, as I always used to do when she was in the final stages of Alzheimer's disease. I made myself a cup of tea, weak green tea, to which I first became addicted in the early hours of the morning when Iris used to wander about downstairs, talking to herself, piling up rubbish, cutlery, cushions, bits of clothing.

She was never difficult or ungentle with me, even then, but it was no use trying to persuade her back to bed until some invisible natural process seemed to summon her to go back there. I used to follow her cautiously upstairs, and when I found her lying in bed and smiling up at me I used to turn her gently on her side, which I knew she liked, tuck her up and kiss her goodnight, although by then it was often four or five in the morning. That was a blessed moment. I did not try to go to sleep then. I felt too wide awake. So I made the tea and wandered about a bit myself, and then went upstairs and lay down beside her, now sweetly and tranquilly asleep. This was my day-dreaming and remembering time, the best time of the day, apart from the happy hour in the evening when I got Iris into bed and kissed her goodnight, and then came down and had two strong drinks and read some old favourite like *Hornblower* or Barbara Pym.

Remembering those days, wishing they weren't over, I went down this morning, ten days after she died, to make my cup of green tea, and I hooked the back of my vest over the arm of the Windsor chair. Surprisingly difficult to put the mug down carefully, turn round and unhook myself. As I did so there fell like a chord of music on my mind the knowledge that I'd done it before, almost exactly a year ago; and that I had meant to tell Iris about it. If I could have made her understand, and even at that stage she could usually understand funny things, I was sure that she would have been amused. But I never told her, because she was asleep, and later on other more pressing matters had driven the incident out of my head.

This time I was determined to tell her. I would carry my mug upstairs and show her how the hole at the back of my vest had got itself hooked on the chair. I was sure she would find it funny when I explained that I had felt like a dog pulling at the lead. At all stages of Alzheimer's, getting jokes across seems of great importance.

I had honestly forgotten for the moment that Iris was dead, and that I shouldn't be able to tell her.

It must have been because the original moment when I had hooked my vest on the chair, a year ago, was still so vivid in my mind.

I could see myself going rather quickly up the stairs, though carrying the mug carefully, and saying, 'Darling, guess what happened.'

I saw myself doing it, and I saw Iris in bed, and beginning to sit up with a smile to hear what I was going to tell her. But she had disappeared before I reached our bedroom.

She wasn't there. She had died in the Home ten days before; yet she seemed to have been with me, at our house, until this moment. My wish to tell her this comic incident of the morning, the thing that had also happened to me a year ago, seemed abruptly to have deprived her of the life which, up to that moment, she had been living in my mind. The joke had vanished with her. There were no more jokes. Because jokes were things that I shared with her.

So I sat down on the bed, drinking my tea, and wondering what I was going to do with the rest of my life.

There is a play by Bernard Shaw called *Widowers' Houses*. I have never seen or read it and have very little idea what it's about. Possibly it's about respectable people who get their income from slum properties; some issue that was then festering away under the skirts of polite society. I recall that he wrote a series called *Plays Pleasant and Unpleasant*. This must have been one of the unpleasant ones.

The title intrigues me, though I shall take no steps to find out more about the play. For me, *Widowers' Houses* are houses with widowers living in them. Like my house. It used to be our house. It is still our bedroom, our garden, our fig-tree, Iris's chair in the garden, over which Virginia creeper has been stealthily growing all last summer. In the autumn the plant would go scarlet, and how passionately I longed for that autumn, and for an end to the long, stale summer days. I think Iris longed for them to be over too. Autumn and winter were our time, and grey days without sun. I hate the sun especially.

For some reason it is not 'our house' any more, but we still seem to have 'our friends' and even 'our Home'. That is Vale House, where Iris died. Tricia O'Leary, who runs it, is very much 'our friend'. The Home is a safe, good, happy place, which Iris loved at once. But when we arrived she wouldn't get out of the taxi until the nurse gently took her fingers. Smiling at her, and walking backwards, she led Iris unresisting to the door, as if they were having a little dance together. In a moment Iris, too, was smiling; and she never looked back.

Vale House was far from being a Vale of Tears. But as I sat in the taxi holding Iris's hand and telling the driver where to go I remembered Mrs Gamp's philosophical observation. 'He were born in a Wale and he lived in a Wale, and he must accept the consequences of his sitivation.'

I must accept them now too, as Iris did.

Although it may be a widower's house, it feels just the same as it was when it was our house. It's not that I haven't 'had the heart' to do anything; it's more that I can't see the point of doing it. Iris's things stay heaped up on the floor, undisturbed. Her dusty spectacles, unworn for several years, lie on the window-ledge, coiled about with the black cord I got for her to hang them round her neck, which she never did. There is a vague drift of objects in the corners of rooms, piled up sometimes to a depth of a foot or more, so that one has to climb over them. Five, six weeks have now gone by, but nothing has been cleared away.

Some day, I suppose, I shall get rid of them all. Some day the house will become a new sort of house, a house for me to occupy.

Iris wrote in the little upstairs room. I don't know what I shall do with that. She wrote six or seven of her novels there, and most of her long philosophical study, *Metaphysics as a Guide to Morals*. I can't remember which novel she was in the middle of when we arrived here, back in 1989.

I have a sudden premonition that the widowed state must ripen and fatten as the months and years go by. Does the past then eat the present, becoming even more powerful, more unruly and seductive? As I try to find new things to do, will the past just smile at me like a big cat, and creep all the closer?

Well, anyway, I remember our arrival here as an exciting moment. I had been fond of our little house in Hartley Road, where we had moved from the country when our old home at Steeple Aston – shabby but rather grand in its way – had begun to feel as if it could tolerate us no longer. The Hartley Road house was on a corner and noisy, but Iris was loyal to it because she knew I had fallen sentimentally in love with the idea of such a house, if not the reality. It was a relief to us both, however, when we had the unexpected chance of moving again.

Our new house was no bigger than Hartley Road and the rooms were pokier, but the little back and front gardens were full of big trees. Brickwalled on two sides, the back garden soon began to show, under our ownership, a fine mass of weeds and undergrowth. Elder, bramble, sapling hazel, chestnut and forsythia, growing thickly up to the back fence, gave an impression of sylvan endlessness. Bluebells had probably always been there, but Queen Anne's Lace now arrived, together with bindweed and dog's mercury, ground elder and deadly nightshade. Two blue cedars that I put in keep state in one corner, and grow a couple of feet every year.

Our small patch of lawn contrasts sprucely with the wilderness. A Russian vine canopies the garage, in which there is everything except a car. Four ornamental conifers, which we used to call the king, the queen and the two princesses, came with us in their tubs from Hartley Road. Replanted in the garden they have shot up like the others. The queen has outgrown her consort and now overtops him by five or six feet. A handsome family.

Iris did sit now and again in the garden chair I got for her, but not very often. I once had a slight qualm when I saw her sitting outside with her exercise book and fountain pen. She looked thoughtful, but not in a good sense. She seemed to be wondering what was happening to her, and finding it something quite outside her experience.

When the chair goes red with the Virginia creeper next autumn and then dulls away into winter, I shall have forgotten how she looked when she sat there. Perhaps I'll take the chair away, because the green plastic chairs I got later at a supermarket are much more practical. More comfortable too. The creeper grew on top of the matted ivy that was making our neighbour's wall so damp, and both had to go. It then grew along the ground and began to entwine itself round the king and queen. I thought it best to pull it off their majesties, but I let it continue to flourish on the teak chair, its only chance of growing upwards. So I'll leave the chair there to turn red next autumn. It's not spring yet, and I hope autumn comes early this year.

At the moment the house – my house – is a refuge rather than a home. A lair. I think of it with longing if I'm forced to go out, and I can't wait to get back again into safety. Once I'm back I at once feel its emptiness, so I go out for one of our little walks – those are still 'ours'. Round the familiar block, and perhaps down to Wolfson College garden and to the middle of the Cherwell bridge where we often used to stand, and sometimes played poohsticks. We never went any further than the middle of the bridge.

Our very old friend Audi, who speaks excellent Spanish having lived in the Canaries for so many years, was once standing there with Iris and a Spanish friend when a punt came under the bridge, creeping sideways and very unadroitly propelled. The friend said to Audi in Spanish, so that he shouldn't be understood by the puntsman: 'That chap's no good. Can't do it for toffee.'

Whereupon the young fellow in the boat looked up and barked back in Spanish, 'It's not so bloody simple as it looks.'

It turned out he came from the Asturias, and he and his fellow-countryman on the bridge exchanged jocular insults as the punt receded crabwise into the distance.

Iris was scornful of the Oxford school of punting. She had learnt to do it at Cambridge when she was a research student at Newnham. She had been refused a visa for America, where she had been awarded a Commonwealth Fellowship, because of her one-time membership of the Communist Party. (Because she had owned up to it, which her former friends, many now in senior government positions, did not, she was automatically debarred from entry to the USA.)

In Cambridge, an Arab philosopher taught her to punt, and she was proud of being able to do it in the Cambridge style. The puntsman stands precariously on the slippery end, instead of on the more safely recessed stern. But I never saw her punt, and I have never done it myself, nor wished to. I liked looking at the young women in punts, as I stood there with Iris, but few of them looked at all ladylike, or were dressed for the part. They wore grubby jeans and many of them were doing the work themselves, often with a fixed sneer of contempt or concentration while the boyfriend lolled on the cushions.

Back to the house again, with the usual feeling of relief and release. Into safety, where I don't have to catch trains, go into college where everyone looks so sympathetic, or be invited out to supper. I don't even have to answer the phone, I can switch it off.

Overgrown as the front garden is, you would hardly guess from the outside of the house what a mass of debris lurks within. When I go to have a pee I notice that even the soap by the bath is dirty. How does it get like that? Disuse? Overuse? Hardly the latter.

It was some time before she died that I gave up trying to get Iris's clothes off, let alone wash her. Like a timid animal to whom it is natural to be as it is, she had begun to shy nervously away from Audi or me, but when she was in the Home, for less than a month as it turned out, she loved being washed, and would sit smiling blissfully as Tricia or Maureen soaped and towelled her. Our friend Peter's angelic partner Jim had this natural gift too, very much like that of a good keeper at a zoo, and Iris loved having him shampoo her hair. Sometimes she uttered eldritch shrieks as he did so, whereupon Jim, with a beaming smile, would shriek back at her, and then both of them would go off together into fits of hearty laughter. But in the last days even Jim could not help her.

Nothing has changed in the bedroom, which is still 'ours'. I am still on my side of the bed, naturally enough. Hotel beds are like this when you arrive: no sign of any previous occupant. But hotel beds get made.

A friend sends a photo taken last year. It's in the kitchen. Like all photographs of house interiors (pictures too, including Vermeer) the room looks more mysterious and more attractive than it really is. Can a photograph show dust, even in the quantities we have it? Hardly. But the walls I painted a warm red nine years ago look warmer and redder in the photo, less faded than they are, and the hugger-mugger of half-full mugs and unwashed plates and saucers appear as positively picturesque, with the look, as T.S. Eliot wrote in a poem, of things 'that are looked at'. On their best behaviour.

Shadowy through the doorway looms the book-mountain. Row upon row of piled-up books have accumulated for years in the narrow passage – review copies, reprints, proof copies, or new novels in their once spotless jackets sent by publishers, or sometimes by the authors themselves. All seem to reproach me, saying they might have been brilliant and wonderful, or at least profoundly interesting and informative, if they had been given their chance. And now they know it's too late. They peer wistfully into the kitchen; they even give me guilt feelings. Now and again I open one, read a few sentences, can't make head or tail of them, put the book back.

Sometimes I have managed to give one away to a visitor. But mostly they sit there hopelessly, the ones towards the bottom with the least hope of all. I should take them to Oxfam, I know, but still they sit there, and still they accrete. Who would want to read them now?

The photo makes the dried marguerite daisies in the Korean vase seem strange, outlandish, almost beautiful. The vase comes from a pottery in Seoul. When we were there once on a cultural visit we were invited to draw on a newly-made vase which was brown and unglazed. I drew a big Russian Ж (*Zh*) – a letter I loved at the time. I was trying to learn some Russian in the cause of my passion for Pushkin's poems.

The vases came to us glazed next day with an exquisite grey sheen; the markings with a dark brown pencil had come out Vermeer blue. Iris preferred to leave her own vase unmarked. It should be in a cupboard somewhere, but where?

Iris faces the camera, her hands on the back of her chair. She looks alert and happy, and is wearing the purple T-shirt Jim once gave her. The logo of a Canadian sports club is stencilled ornately on the front. On her shoulder sits the little yellow Teletubby someone else gave her. Members of a savage tribe, if savage tribes still exist, would assume at once that the little creature is the Alzheimer demon. A palpable emanation, surprised here by the camera.

Looking at the photo, I think of the last page of Iris's last novel, *Jackson's Dilemma*. Jackson is sitting on the grass feeling that life is over. 'He thought, my power has left me, will it ever return? … At the end of what is necessary I have come to a place where there is no road.' Jackson haunts me. So does the picture of him on the jacket. He looms there in a shadowy half-transparent way, concerned, unhappy, but always well-wishing, and as if about to disappear for good. I see from the note that it was drawn by a lady called Liz Cooke. I feel a momentary urge to get in touch with Liz Cooke, wherever she is, and ask what she thought about Jackson, and why she drew him like that.

Jackson is a baffling character. Also a strangely successful one. The reader believes in his powers, his benevolence, his capacity to help others without, apparently, needing to do more to help himself. He is good rather than nice or potent or wonderful. An Irish monk, who came once or twice to visit Iris, courteously disagreed when I suggested that Jackson might be Iris's own inner sense of what was beginning to happen to her. Did Jackson embody 'the end of what is necessary', death, that cannot but be good? We all share in it. The monk, however, would have none of this. For him, Jackson was the Holy Spirit, *tout court*, which Iris's genius as a writer had found and served, even though she was never a conscious believer.

None the less at the end of the book Jackson has lost his powers, but his obscure serenity remains. On the last page he rescues a spider. Iris would have done that, at any stage of her illness.

In the last sentence he smiles, as Iris smiled on the day she died.

I don't like going into the room she wrote in. It is still 'her' room. But it doesn't look as if she could ever have been in 'her room'. Or anybody else for that matter. Her room looks now as if it had already been abandoned long before we came here.

There is a copy of *Jackson's Dilemma* on the floor, which I pick up. The floor is thick with single shoes, and socks, and pieces of the *Evening Standard*, which she used to bring home after she had been up to London. I pick a bit off the floor – already the paper is turning a brownish colour – and find the date. 5 February 1994. About a year before the Alzheimer's started unmistakably to declare itself. No, not so much as a year; more like five or six months.

Iris was always fond of the *Evening Standard*, particularly the comic strips – Modesty Blaise being her favourite. I don't think she ever identified with the exploits of that redoubtable female, but, unconsciously perhaps, she liked to see a woman who was really very 'womanly' (not a word Iris at all cared for) behaving with such supermasculine vigour and resolution. Up to the time she ceased reading altogether she looked at the paper for Modesty's sake. I managed to get it for her most days by going down to the railway station, the only place it was available in Oxford. I would make a little routine of our driving down together, and she would sit in the car while I nipped in to buy it at the bookstall. I, too, followed the adventures of Modesty, although I could not see her as a woman at all and she had no part in my sex day-dreams. Iris said she liked the absence of sex. 'Same as in *Treasure Island*?' I asked, and Iris emphatically agreed. Stevenson was a favourite of her father's, and *Treasure Island* was read to her when she was five or six.

Writing about his father, John Mortimer records that his last words were 'I'm always angry when I'm dying', and adds that these seemed like words that his father – a barrister in the Probate, Divorce and Admiralty Division – might have been preparing to say for some time. In any case they are just right; and yet they are the words of an actor, which all barristers have, to some extent, to be. Iris had no last words, which was natural in her circumstances, but also she didn't have to be any sort of an actor.

In fact we both much disliked the theatre, though my dislike of it was more vocal than that of Iris, who without pretending was always polite and deferential about theatre business, as she was to her actor acquaintances and friends. But if we had to go to the theatre, she had, just as I did, that awful mixture of boredom and embarrassment that natural non-theatre-goers feel about the whole thing. It is like being tone-deaf.

Shakespeare is not exempt from this tone-deaf reaction in Iris and me: in fact he is, quite involuntarily of course, the prime offender. To read him, to recall the words of his beings in the mind's eye – that is one thing. To see the poor man 'acted' is, for us, quite another. We would rather pay a large sum than have to sit through *King Lear*; and we would do anything to avoid a 'sparkling performance' of Rosalind in *As You Like It*, or Beatrice in *Much Ado*.

For more than thirty years we managed to avoid Stratford altogether, except for one occasion when we were staying with the Priestleys, who lived nearby. Most uncharacteristically, for although a playwright he was no great devotee of the theatre, the Bard least of all, Priestley had taken seats for us to see Peter O'Toole as Shylock. After that experience we recovered over dinner in the sumptuous atmosphere of Kissing-Tree House, where Jack's expert staff had been devoted to him for many years.

By no means an untalkative man, Jack made no comment on the performance or play, but as he poured us out a bottle to go with the smoked salmon, he remarked: 'The quality of Meursault is not strained.'

It was indeed delicious Meursault, but I couldn't help wondering if, as in the case of Mortimer's father, the jest mightn't have been some time in preparation.

No more than actors are playwrights spontaneous people, but whereas actors have to pretend to be, writers and their audience are well aware how much midnight oil has been burnt, and can savour the results accordingly, like connoisseurs of a fine wine. Shakespeare's happiest things can *seem* to come off the cuff – to the envy of Dryden and Ben Jonson – but as with all verbal art, appearances can be misleading.

Jack was much attached to Iris; he called her 'Ducky' and advised her in a fatherly way when she tried turning some of her novels into plays. He co-wrote with her the play *A Severed Head*, producing a number of new jokes, all of which, as even I had to admit, came off delightfully in the theatre. I remarked as much to Jack, who told me that things that are not funny at all when you merely say them, like 'Did you find a parking space?' could, by means of context and timing, become hilarious on the lips of a really good actor. For us theatrically-challenged persons that is the only thing an actor is really good for.

To my surprise I was not in the least embarrassed by Iris's plays, and in fact rather enjoyed them, particularly *The Servants and the Snow*, which was turned into an opera by William Matthias. One of its sad little arias still haunts my ear. Although not tone-deaf about music, Iris and I had no more inner sense and true grasp of it than we had of the theatre. Although Jack did such a brilliant job on *A Severed Head*, Iris's other plays are all rather lacking in excitement, a fact she was well aware of herself, and quite unbothered about. She knew the theatre wasn't her thing, but why shouldn't she have a try occasionally? It interested and amused her, and did no one any harm.

For me this introduces one of life's little ironies, only discoverable after a death. Bereavement has to be acted. Living now in my widower's house it is no use saying I'm tone-deaf theatrically, for widowers are compelled to be actors; they have no choice. Naturally all of us are always acting a bit, acting the part of ourselves; but when we acquire a new profession – still more a new status – a new kind of role is required. At first I played a teacher of English, then a retired teacher of English. Not difficult to get the hang of that sort of part.

Playing a relict, or bereaved husband, is rather more demanding, but in an absurd sense more rewarding too. That acute, if tiresome, old theologian Von Hügel remarked that one kissed one's child not only because one loved it, but *in order that* one might love it. Does that sound like Teutonic overkill, or to put it in more Anglo-Saxon terms, a belt-and-braces policy? Going through the motions in order to feel the right emotions.

Getting a letter from anyone who has written good – as opposed to those merely conventional – words of condolence, such as 'our thoughts are with you at this difficult time', I find a helpless and involuntary spasm of tears prickling at my eyelids, while my face contracts like that of a disappointed baby. These symptoms have to be sternly repressed in public, and a properly controlled portion of restrained lachrymosity put in their place. At this stage I remember how the young David Copperfield, all of eight or nine years old, learned his own part as a bereaved child. He stood on a chair in the schoolroom to see with satisfaction how red his eyes were; and this in a sense had nothing to do directly with the depth and desolation of his grief at his mother's death. It was a way of revealing it, and so of coming to terms with it. Crafty old Von Hügel may have detested his offspring, if indeed he had any, but he perceived that by playing his part correctly he would come to feel the right thing about them. No hypocrisy in that. 'Being is acting,' says one of Iris's characters.

So I play my part. And really, it is hard to distinguish at moments between playing the part of one who is bereft, and one who suffers all the inward misery of bereavement.

None of this acting business applied when I was a 'carer'. There was no one then before whom to play the part. Not even myself. For the first time in my life I suppose, and it must apply to all the rest of us 'carers' too, I found myself in what seemed the truly natural state of man, doing not what I wanted to do but what had to be done: sinking into daily depression; flying into rages; knowing wild moments of the purest relief and elation when I loved Iris more than I had ever done before, and felt closer to her than I had ever felt before...

*

That was the end of what I wrote down just after Iris died, and apparently forgot about in the days that followed. The two women and the time I had had with them had driven it out of my head.

I sat at the kitchen table and pondered the pages. I decided it must have cheered me up to write them. I decided it would do me good now to go on writing. I realised, in an indifferent way, how extremely self-centred I seemed to have become. With Iris gone there was no other centre. Anything I wrote would just be about myself now. That could not be helped: or at least I was not going to do anything to help it.

Margot and Mella had certainly been a distraction. To start writing again now would at least be a substitute for Mella's departure. Should I write now about the time I had had with the pair of them, and the drama – for surely it was no less than that? – of their meeting?

I decided not to. Perhaps I had the feeling, even the wish, that the drama might not yet be over. Mella might return. Perhaps I half hoped she would.

I might as well start again from the point – more or less – where I had left off: that morning quite soon after Iris died. Probably now that Mella had disappeared, and there was little news of Margot, nothing much more would happen. Part of me – most of me – hoped it would not. That must be, surely, the way I still wanted my new life to become? And to remain.

PART II

CHAPTER SIX

Back to Words and Books

I still have a sensation – no doubt all widows and widowers know it? – of being dead and buried. In the grave beside the loved one, like the deceased who might or might not have been a keen gardener. A rather grotesque sensation, putting one in the same place too as Hardy's wife, or his dog, or the other denizens of that buried world that he liked in his poems to imagine as still capable of being in touch with the living. They recall us at moments, and wave to us, and it is a satisfaction for them to think of us there, under the ground, separated but together. And not unseparated, even if we are in the form of ashes – the ashes of incinerated bones weigh quite a bit apparently – and scattered over the fields, or in the sea …

Suppose one were to become the unknown skeleton, hanging in a dusty corner of the anatomy department? Odd how difficult it would be to feel 'together yet separated' from a skeleton, even that of a loved one whose identity was known. At this point matters become too Gothic. In *The Revenger's Tragedy*, a Jacobean play now thought to be by Middleton, if I remember rightly, and not by Tourneur as was once supposed, the hero carried his fiancée's skull about with him. He does this to remind him to avenge her murder, but it would be a bit like knowing whose skeleton it was in the corner of the lab.

Since I've left myself to science in my will, as Iris did, I could easily end up as such a skeleton. Half of me might belong to some medical student. Peter Conradi told me that when he started off in medicine (he gave it up later) he temporarily owned such a half, bargaining it from a needy fellow student for whisky and cigarettes.

Hardy might easily have written a poem – perhaps not one of his best – about such a skeleton, hanging in a corner of the anatomy

113

department, and lamenting to the poet that in the pride of enlightened middle age, when death is unimaginable, he had left himself to science. How bitterly he now regrets it as he hangs in his dusty corner!

I remembered asking the undertaker about coffins. I already knew from an official on the phone that Iris would have to be cremated or buried. After taking samples of her brain they were, for some reason, not permitted to make the rest of her over to the anatomy department.

Was it necessary to have a coffin, I asked. The undertaker looked unsurprised and a little weary, as if this was just one of the ways by which his customers hoped to reduce the bill, and he had heard them all many times.

'Coffin? Not for the interment, sir.'

I must have looked surprised, because he went on to explain that, strictly speaking, all that was technically necessary for an interment was a shroud. Cremation, on the other hand, required a coffin. This seemed to me illogical, but there was no point in saying so. Instead I was tempted to ask what difference it made to the price. But I didn't feel up to trying to tease him. It was clear, in any case, that he was impervious to being teased. He anticipated any query I might have raised.

'Expenses, sir, are very similar, unless you should be requiring something quite out of the ordinary.'

I wondered what sort of thing I could suggest: perhaps a silver birch or a gingko (Iris's favourite tree) planted on the site of the grave or ashes. But again, in his slightly uncanny fashion, the undertaker seemed to anticipate the direction in which my mind was working. Should I have ecology in mind, he assured me, the plain wooden coffin was kinder to nature than the composition substitute. He did not explain why, and again I did not feel up to asking him. I wanted now to end the interview as soon as possible. But something about it made me suddenly determined to change my will. Previously I had been convinced that I couldn't care less about my own disposal, but something about the undertaker now made me think again. I felt relieved and grateful that Iris, apart from the samples of her brain in

various places of learning, was to be safely incinerated. I determined
to follow her example.

Nor need I be present, as the undertaker was now reassuring me,
when Iris was cremated. The job would be done at the quiet time in
the early morning; before the rush, so to speak. I was glad of that. And
I was glad I had decided not to be an official skeleton. I must
remember to change my will.

I thought of the skeleton I would escape becoming, its bony arms
and legs manipulated expertly by a demonstrator, or jocosely by idle
students. The thought of it brought me back to the moment on that
Monday afternoon in Vale House. Iris had seemed a little uncomfort-
able on her back, and I settled her on her side where she lay quietly at
ease, her eyes open. She reached her arms out and began to move them
to and fro as if playing. Perhaps she was indeed playing a game, the
rules of which would never be explained. Patting her hands I tried to
play with her, but her arms were like well-designed mechanical
devices, which did not resist my hand, but as soon as released resumed
their purposeful continuity, to and fro, to and fro.

There began to be something perturbing about these movements,
which bore no relation to the games we used to play together.
Remembering now their strange softness and gentleness I thought of
Dr Jacoby, that kind scholar and brain specialist, who used to drop in
on us from time to time when the Alzheimer's was entering its final
stages. After Iris died he told me that our brains are made of a very
soft, almost jelly-like, material. To be studied under the microscope
they must first be 'fixed' in formalin, a delicate and complex process
which takes weeks, perhaps months, to complete in the pathology lab.

Through this softness in the head all the infinite complexity of
physical and mental behaviour is transmitted and controlled. Was this
movement of Iris's arms all that was left of the mysteries within a once
brilliant brain? 'I intend to make my mark,' the young Iris had once
said, long before I met her.

Her genius lives in her books, but that brilliant brain will continue,
strangely enough, to have its own sort of physical existence.

I remembered turning Iris gently on to her other side, and as I moved her I realised that she was no longer there. She had stopped breathing. And she had done it as naturally as the rest of us carry on breathing. I held her hands now and they remained, as if trustfully, in mine. I closed her eyes and then opened them again as if I were myself playing a little game with her; and when I opened them she looked at me, as if merrily, and as if she were glad that I was still there.

I was glad too. I should always have been sorry if I had not been there. I would have felt like a bird-watcher who had been absent, or looking the wrong way, and had missed the brief appearance of a rare and wonderful bird.

That sense of exaltation soon disappeared. And soon, too, there were all the 'arrangements' to be made. It was perhaps because I was still feeling the effects of being exalted that I had the idea of teasing the professionally unteasable undertaker. A big, solidly-built man, who looked like my idea of a Victorian archdeacon. He wore a curious sleeveless waistcoat of black padded nylon, which seemed thoroughly suitable as a kind of 'undress' style for calling on clients on a cold day, although not, of course, for the pomp and circumstance of the funeral. His manner was equally calm and reassuring. We will take care of everything; all you have to do is pay the bill. Which I had done, on the spot, and without a murmur.

*

A widower after forty-four years, or however much more it is. I don't feel strong enough at the moment to tot the months up. I only feel strong enough to go on writing about Iris, which means writing about ourselves – myself. G.K. Chesterton said that if a man ceases to believe in God he doesn't believe in nothing – he believes in anything. I cling to writing as a form of belief. I don't believe in anything else, but I believe in Iris, and believing in her is a belief in her survival, both for me in my own way, and for her survival in everyone who reads her work. How could I not believe that?

I'm like Hardy believing in his wife, Emma, surviving on the wild North Cornish shore and on the cliff-top where she used to ride her pony. Emma surviving and talking to him, telling him she was not as she was ... But Iris for me is just as she was, whether before or after the Alzheimer's; although I know that her survival for me depends on me, that we shall soon pass into 'existlessness' together, and that Iris will then remain alive only for her readers down the years and the ages.

> It shall not last for ever,
> No more than earth or skies ...

as Housman says; but at least it will last as long as there are books to read.

I thought of Jake in Iris's first novel, *Under the Net*, riding on top of a bus and thinking of death. Thoughts come and go; they are used and they are enjoyed, and they vanish with the last chop which ends them. 'So I meditated, and was reluctant to get off the bus.' Had Iris lost all thoughts before she died? Again I can't stop thinking of that once active, fertile brain darkening, emptying, going dim and void ... And as so often when she was alive, I don't know whether or not to hope that through that dark time there was nothing there.

What can one mean by a brain with nothing there? It sounds peaceful, even merciful, and yet of course it isn't. There was the unending anxiety of Alzheimer's. During the last few months, when the incoherence that goes with anxiety began to dissipate at last, Iris could not think. But she could feel, act on impulse, even plan. Anxiety as a state of mind was replaced by an occasional, but purposeful, impulse to escape. To try the door until the moment came when I had forgotten to relock it after we had come in together, and then to run out and disappear from the oppressions of the mind and its emptiness, and the house and its emptiness. She could no longer fill it with her love and purpose and all their activities. Love had lost its purpose and remained only as itself, the impulse that still made her throw herself into my arms, but could shed no tears for us, nor look into my eyes.

To escape. Anywhere, anywhere out of the world. Not into death, for clearly death as an idea no longer existed. Iris no longer had any awareness of it.

Or had she? At Vale House in the last month she was happy. No need for escape now. Her body seemed to know that death was coming and became glad; her smiles in reply to the nurses' smiles more rapturous. She smiled at us all as if she were giving a party. That she did not, or could not, eat or drink was for her a bit of a joke, about which she was half apologetic, and a little mischievous too. Yet no one in Vale House thought she was going to die so soon.

Her body wished to be finished with itself. Those reachings out of her arms seemed like a rite of departure. And then she was gone. Broncho-pneumonia, said the death certificate: the standard conventional formula. But an elderly body cannot last long without food or water, and the body seems to know this well.

I keep coming back to it all and mixing up experiences in a chaotic way. But I must become coherent; settle down in my new widower's house, put the rooms and myself in order. In several places, on the floors of rooms or in a pile of miscellaneous objects, I see Jackson's beautiful haunting face, the face on the jacket of Iris's last novel.

'My powers have left me, will they return? At the end of what is necessary I have come to a place where there is no road.'

Jackson is there; but so many things that used to be in the house seem to have disappeared. Suddenly remembering the Korean vase, one of the pair we were given in Seoul, I started the other day to search for it compulsively. She said she liked the plain grey. But perhaps if I could only find it there would be a message on it for me, some tranquil blue letters which would speak to me alone?

It was no use. I looked everywhere. But the vase had gone.

All right, let all the things in the house disappear, unremembered and unrecorded, without my having to do anything further about them. Let them all vanish and be no more seen, so that I can start again. But for the bereft, remembering becomes as much of an obsession as first love once was.

I loved Iris when she was writing, and far off from me. As a writer she was always spare, quiet, intent. A very private writer, who seldom showed me anything at the time she was writing. And I never asked her. All that was outside ourselves, and our own life together. Now I read her books the whole time; and writing of her – with her as it seems – is the only way of communicating I still have.

No wonder Hardy held those dialogues in poetry with his dead wife Emma. They drifted apart – really apart, not closer apart. He didn't talk to her much when she was alive, and he seems not to have talked to his second wife Florence either. Communication for him was his poetry, the mode through which he learnt – after her death – to talk to Emma. For a reticent man, too, it was a way of communing with himself.

I never felt that that was true of Iris. The self she was with me was not the self who wrote, but she never seemed to commune with any other self in her own writing either. One odd reason why the characters in Hardy's novels are often unsatisfactory is that they are outside himself. Iris's were all inside her. Hardy's own inside being comes out only in his poetry; he always regarded himself as a poet who wrote novels for the money. In poetry he leads his own life, and talks with himself as he wishes. His own little fantasies, which often come out in poems, are quite ordinary. He might have married someone else; he might have been a swell gent, or a landowner, or a beautiful woman or a singing bird. But for him as for Yeats, a very different kind of poet, words themselves are the true good, the certain comforter.

Much more so, I myself find nowadays, than fantasies are. Nowadays, I have fantasies with words. They get nowhere, and would have very little public appeal, but they absorb me in some familial way, for I find myself explaining them to Iris, who lends an indulgent ear. I wouldn't, of course, have bothered her with them when she was alive and well and busy.

As the poet Auden wisely observed, 'Memorable Words' is the only good definition of poetry. He himself when he was young loved geological terms like 'iron pyrites'.

I have learnt a few words of Spanish, mostly of the useful kind, which for that reason are the ones that are hardest to remember. The only one of these that has really stuck means our plain and humble little 'too', which no one could consider putting in any category of memorableness.

But the Spanish *demasiado* – there is a lordly 'too', with a fine full distinction, a word under full sail! *'Demasiado caliente!'* I imagine myself observing tersely but graciously to some chambermaid, as I step into the high hot bath she has prepared for me. She will hasten to run in some cold water, giving me occasion to tell her a few moments later, *'Ahora demasiado frio!'* It would make my day.

This kind of fantasy has no linguistic boundaries, particularly if one knows very few of the words in a language, and none of the grammar. In 1993, Iris and I were conveyed in a ramshackle Russian van from the city to Moscow airport, in company with Sir Michael Caine, promoter of the Russian Booker Prize; an enterprising venture which was having its first trial that year. Although she had once studied Russian, Iris in her modest way declined to take part, but she was warmly pressed by Sir Michael, who had become very fond of her, to come along anyway to grace the judging ceremony. Like many incompetent linguists, including, by his own claim, Edward Lear, I can read – up to a point – without properly understanding a language or being able to speak it. This is true of my Russian. I love the words, but learnt them only from Pushkin's poems, bits of which I know by heart. This hardly constituted a reason for being a junior member of the Booker jury committee, but Sir Michael seemed to think it enough; and I struggled with the (fortunately meagre) number of novels offered by sceptical Russian publishers for our attention. The list had already been weeded out by native critics. We duly made an award, which seemed reasonably just as well as popular, letting ourselves be guided by the masterful Chairwoman, a former high-up in the Communist Party educational system. One of the books on offer she had viewed with great severity, pronouncing it a novel too disgusting even to read. This verdict mildly surprised the American juror as well as myself, as both of us were well accustomed to much worse things in our perusal of contemporary Western fiction. But Russian novelists had recently drunk the uncensored draught of sexual liberty, and had become touchingly determined to demonstrate that today in the former Soviet Union anything goes. With the usual results.

The ceremony that followed was not without some tricky moments. The assembled guests, having drunk a good quantity of vodka, seemed unaware that Sir Michael was making a rather good speech to them in English; they paid no attention to the translation which followed, but continued to dispute the award among themselves with some heat, and at the tops of their voices.

Next morning we set off for the airport in a van which seemed about to break down at any moment. The only thing that worked well was the heating, which was super-efficient, but as it happened the early November weather was uncommonly warm. On our first visit, more than a month before, it had snowed and frozen so hard that the planes on the runway had had to be de-iced. We were appropriately clad for an arctic Moscow, not for this unexpected and overpowering heatwave.

After we had endured it for a few minutes, Sir Michael turned to me and said, 'John, tell him to open the window and switch the bloody heating off. I'm being boiled.'

There was no Russian in the van, or an interpreter to help me out. I had a moment of utter blankness, and then two words from Pushkin popped into my head as if by magic, as magically indeed as the wonderful events in his poem *Ruslan and Lyudmila*. I turned to the driver and said in what I hoped was a lofty and authoritative tone:

'*Slishkom teplo.*'

The sallow woebegone face of the young driver, who looked like an old-fashioned English spiv and was dressed for the part, turned its gaze on me in some surprise. I had a moment of panic. Were Pushkin's words wholly obsolete, poetical, old-fashioned, entirely devoid of contemporary meaning? ... But then with suddenly respectful haste, the driver fiddled with something on his antique dashboard. An irregular roaring, which we had hardly heard above the noise of the van traversing the ravines and crevasses in the Moscow suburban boulevard, ceased abruptly. With a sweep of his arm the driver forced

121

down the window, and within seconds the temperature was back to normal, indeed rather below it.

Pushkin had saved the day. I had a quick mental picture of his dark good-natured face and his famous flashing white teeth, smiling at me with puckish amusement. But anxieties instantly returned. Suppose Sir Michael now felt too cold and asked me to have the window closed, and the heating restored? I searched my mind for a word-spell that might do this, but nothing came. Iris gave me a comforting smile and a squeeze, but I remained on tenterhooks until we bumped past the last of the scraggy birches and into Sheremetyev airport. After uttering my majestic announcement I was further distracted by the young driver, who kept up a one-sided conversation, presumably taking for granted that 'too hot' was not the only Russian phrase I knew. He seemed to have taken quite a fancy to me. I laughed heartily at what he said to try to show I was in the picture, and occasionally uttered a 'Da' or a 'Horosho', but I hadn't the faintest idea what he was talking about, and I was relieved to get to the airport without too much loss of face.

Slishkom teplo! Demasiado caliente! These lordly phrases seem to speak to one another from opposite ends of Europe, almost unattached to their meanings, but sharing that ring of zestful exactness which goes with the words of which poetry can be made.

When in Pushkin's heroic poem *Poltava* the young Cossacks dismiss the wily old Mazeppa as being too old to lead them – *on slishkom star!* – the words give the feeling of poetry springing freshly from the page, uncreated before. It seems as scornfully *slishkom* as it is possible to be. Pushkin only uses simple words in his poems; but he uses them as if such words had never been used before, and had never before possessed the force and magic of meaning which his poetry now gives them.

Since Iris died poems and bits of poems float into my head at all hours, in place of those little 'soap fantasies' that used to run there, sometimes rewinding themselves and reappearing in a slightly different version. But now pieces of poem come when I get out of bed, or when the disturbed and disturbing emptiness of mid-morning seems all that the day offers. These poem-words not only console more than my soap fantasies ever did, but seem to wander about in the head and out of it, like the thoughts which Belial in *Paradise Lost* says are the chief consolation of consciousness, of being alive.

> For who would lose
> Though full of pain, this intellectual being,
> These thoughts that wander through eternity,
> To perish rather, swallowed up and lost
> In the wide womb of uncreated night,
> Devoid of sense and motion.

When Iris was alive I often thought of Belial's words, and of the horror in her poor head, where thoughts no longer hovered about like dust motes in the mind's sunlight.

Or did they? How could we be sure, who could say? Was it just that she had no means of letting me know? Is the expression of our experience inseparable from experience itself, as I think we unconsciously assume and take for granted? If we feel or think something we cannot help but express it in some form, in our heads or to other people: the one following from the other.

Critics have suggested the possibility that Milton, writing that passage in *Paradise Lost*, had in mind, or at least in his unconscious memory, the speech in Shakespeare's *Measure for Measure* in which Lucio, under sentence of death, expresses so dramatically the terror of losing all that comes to us with our consciousness.

> Aye, but to die and go we know not where,
> To lie in cold obstruction and to rot ...
> This sensible warm motion to become
> A kneaded clod, and the delighted spirit
> To bathe in fiery floods, or to reside
> In thrilling region of thick-ribbed ice ...

Never mind the fire and ice that once went with hell and purgatory.

123

What strikes home now in the passage is our precarious possession of a 'delighted spirit', and its 'sensible warm motion'. No: we can't leave that, whatever happens. Not until we absolutely have to.

It seems likely that both passages may derive, perhaps independently, from that little poem supposed to have been written by the Emperor Hadrian; perhaps written when he was himself near death.

> *animula vagula blandula*
> *hospes comesque corporis*
> *quo nunc abibis? in loca*
> *pallidula rigida nubila*
> *nec ut soles dabis iocos*

> little mind, tender little wanderer,
> body's guest and companion,
> where must you be off to now? into a place
> dark enough, and rigid and gloomy,
> nor will you exchange familiar jokes.

Translation, however inadequate, at least shows the similarity with those other examples. The mind, like the body, is warm and tender, but until it dies and disappears with the body it can wander about as the body cannot, cherishing itself, and its thoughts, and its joke-pleasures.

If examples like this are anything to go by, the Roman sense of humour remains quite familiar to us. Those customary or habitual jokes and comic rituals must go on in most homes, now as then. Their usualness can become wearisome, but is also a part of their power to comfort, like those 'situation' jokes which recur week by week in the *New Yorker*; the cowled figure with a scythe over his shoulder who appears at the door of the matrimonial apartment, or (as used to be) the Charles Addams family spreading their own peculiar forms of sweetness and light.

A truly new joke is the greatest of rarities, but possibly the Emperor Vespasian, one of Hadrian's predecessors, made such a joke when by accident or design he exclaimed on his deathbed '*ut puto deus fio*' – 'I rather think I'm becoming a god.' Deification after death was a normal part of the imperial procedure, but Vespasian, toughest of tough eggs – and with his son Titus the destroyer of Jerusalem – might seem on the face of it the last person not to take himself quite seriously, even as he lay dying. His remark might of course have been made in all seriousness, but it doesn't sound like it. It is disconcerting to think that ogres and tyrants (and possibly Vespasian was neither) may have just as much ability to see a joke, or to make one at their own expense, as we would wish to think we had ourselves. That said, it is none the less hard to imagine Hitler or Stalin making or enjoying a merry quip about their failing powers, or their ultimate destiny.

As it happens A.E. Housman the poet and Adolf Hitler the monster had the same sort of sense of humour – crude, vulgar, scatological and unfunny. But there don't seem to be any conclusions to be drawn from that. Iris disliked sex jokes except the really elegant and witty ones. Sex is a subject about which the humorist is well advised to go carefully and to tread delicately – not usually a recipe for successful joke-making, nor for the sudden burst of quaint inspiration which caused the emperor Vespasian to observe that he felt he might be on the verge of becoming a god.

*

Thinking about the Russian Booker Prize (now alas defunct) and those fine old muscular words *slishkom* and *demasiado*, led me back to the following year, 1994, and the English Booker Prize. The five of us on the panel had four or five hundred novels to get through – perhaps more, memory does not recall the exact amount – and there was no question of their numbers being weeded out for us; we had to do the whole job ourselves, with three or four months to do it in. I found myself in a state of dazed enjoyment, as book after book, all fresh and optimistic in their gleaming jackets, abode their destined hours in my company, and went their way. A select few were retained beside me for further consultation.

It was books, books, books from morning to night. I asked one or two friends if they would mind reading a few about which I was both interested and doubtful; but with one exception I did not inflict any on Iris, who was just completing *Jackson's Dilemma*. (This was a year or so before the first signs of Alzheimer's disease became fully apparent.) Iris had herself been on the shortlist for the Booker many times, and she won it in 1978 with *The Sea! The Sea! Jackson's Dilemma*, her last offering, appeared in 1995. Its predecessor, *The Green Knight*, had come out at the end of 1993 and was eligible for the 1994 prize. My colleagues were enthusiastic about it, but we all agreed, sensibly I think, that a previous winner should be considered ineligible, at least unofficially. (This sound *ad hoc* convention was not observed when J. M. Coetzee – or was it some other novelist like Salman Rushdie? – was given the prize a second time.)

I had no need to declare an interest in *The Green Knight*; my relation to Iris was obvious. But it happened that my own novel, *Alice*, my first for many years, appeared in June 1994. The publisher said he would have liked to put it in for the prize, but agreed that in the circumstances this was hardly possible. *Alice* was a small *jeu d'esprit* which I had much enjoyed writing; and Colin Haycraft, kindest of men, who ran Duckworth on a shoe-string, said he would be delighted to publish it, provided I did not expect to get paid.

Another colleague, James Wood, caused a slight hitch in our deliberations, upon which the press descended with their usual glee. His wife, like mine, had a novel in for the prize, and he had had the good idea of keeping quiet about this until he had heard the candid comments, arrived at all unawares, from his fellow-members of the jury; for at our joint sessions we briefly discussed each offering. At that crucial point he was planning to modestly observe that the lady whose novel we were talking about happened to be his wife.

But unfortunately another juror got wind of the connection, and taxed James with it before we came to discuss the book, which as it turned out we had all enjoyed, although no one suggested putting it on the shortlist. It was a small matter, although the press inevitably made as much of it as they could. For some reason these Booker goings-on are always newsworthy, and the journalists were delighted when we got ourselves into another muddle over the final selection, ending up with a winner – James Kelman's *How Late It Was, How Late* – which none of us particularly wanted. I was unable to press very hard for my own favourite, Alan Hollinghurst's *The Folding Star*, because that delightful writer had been a pupil of mine when he was doing his thesis at Oxford. Our most spirited juror, Rabbi Julia Neuberger, protested vigorously against our eventual award, taking much the same stand against an 'obscene' novel that our Russian Chairwoman had taken in Moscow the previous year.

Obscenity apart – and the obscenity certainly became monotonous and even ritualised – James Kelman's offering was in its own way a remarkable book, and I do not think we were so wrong in thinking well of it, even though not to the point of wanting it to win. One of our number was strongly in favour of a curious work whose name I cannot now recall, which the author had published herself. It was a religious allegory, set in an imaginary rather than a historical past, and I asked Iris if she would like to have a look at it, since the book certainly made an impression. Iris was impressed too, reading it with characteristic care (the reason why I did not inflict more than this unusual one of my bunch upon her) and making some shrewd comments and criticism. It was less than a year before the early symptoms of Alzheimer's were bad enough to make reading all but impossible for her.

The Booker Prize gives good service to the reading public, and the publicity that surrounds it is not necessarily a bad thing. Martin Goff, the humorous and extremely competent Director who used to run the show, told me that the Board were delighted by the amount of dissension and controversy that went on that year.

'They all agreed, John, that you were the most incompetent Chairman ever, and that this had been a most *excellent* thing.'

On the more serious side, Booker judges can point to uniquely good writers, like Anita Brookner and Penelope Fitzgerald, who won the prize in their uncertain early days, and went on to produce many mature masterpieces. Such an award can give a promising and original writer the best kind of practical encouragement.

*

I keep remembering the day, ages ago now, when I repeated the mantrap episode, catching my tail on the Windsor chair. The way in which the repetition made me forget that Iris was dead was certainly remarkable. I really did think I should be able to tell her what had happened. And it was a bit later that day that I had my first real explosion of tears, as unexpected as a sudden cloudburst or a flash flood. I felt myself borne along on top of it, as one might be on fast flowing water, but the sensation of helplessness was compellingly comforting and engrossing. I couldn't help thinking that it must be rather like the female orgasm, which has been compared to a waterfall. Perhaps it's the only occasion when a male gets some notion of what female experience can be like.

But weeping itself is a solitary experience. Men do it as much as women, but both sexes are secretly indifferent to the other's tears. To be 'a good cry' it must be done on one's own. Otherwise it cannot avoid looking done for a purpose. Tennyson's Princess had no choice but to weep in public, but being used to that she could also be spontaneous. Tennyson the Victorian certainly knew all about it. Home they bring her warrior dead, and she remains expressionless and dry-eyed. What can her maidens do to make her weep?

> Rose a nurse of ninety years,
> Set her babe upon her knee.
> Like summer tempests came her tears.
> 'Sweet my child, I live for thee.'

A fairly accurate account, minus the child in my case of course. But perhaps that mantrap story I so much wanted to tell Iris was a kind of substitute for that cathartic nurse and child?

A quotation from that song in the poem was used by Kenneth

Grahame, rather oddly but successfully, as almost everything in *The Wind in the Willows* is successful. 'Like summer tempests came his tears' became the heading for the last chapter. They are Toad's tears of remorse. Toad – so terminally if so very improbably – has turned over a new leaf. 'He was indeed an altered Toad.' It is as good a way to end the immortal fantasy as any other could be. But summer tempest tears do not herald a new beginning. They hold only belated recognition of what is past.

Iris used to hum her own kind of Toad songs, and she continued to do this after she became ill.

Wow-wer-wer-wow-wow-wow
Wow-wowo-wer-wow-wow-wow

Sometimes, when she could no longer speak at all coherently, she would hum her tune as we lay in bed together in the early morning. In earlier days I used to play our record of the ballet music of *Petrushka*, and Iris loved the bit near the beginning, which we imagined must be the puppet ballerina dancing her *pas seul* for the Moor. We used to hum it together.

WOW-wowo-wow-wow
Wow-wowo-wer-wow-wow-wow

trying to end on that little note of hesitancy and interrogation which is interrupted by new and threatening chords. Together with the later tune from the fairground, which I always thought of as 'Sorochintsy Fair', though that is a tale by Gogol – Stravinsky's is the big annual fair at St Petersburg – we liked it the best of the music in *Petrushka*.

I remember now reading somewhere, or perhaps I heard it on a Radio 3 programme, that Stravinsky 'borrowed' what we thought of as the tune of the little ballerina from a barrel organ which was playing outside his hotel in Paris. To his surprise and annoyance, the composer of this tune – a popular cabaret song – turned out to be very much alive, and recognised it at once when the music of *Petrushka* was

129

publicly recorded. His agent promptly sued Stravinsky for infringe-
ment of copyright, and the great composer had to pay up.

With Iris's little tune often in my head, I recognise it for the first
time as her own memory of *Petrushka*. Emphasised and simplified, her
wow-wows approximate to the tune we used to try to hum together.

I think Iris never tried to compose music, though she had a few
piano lessons when she was small, and at the age of seven or so she
wrote a fairy play for performance by her school class. It had a chorus
of rabbits. So far as I could gather, the rabbits didn't have much to do
except caper about in their furry costumes, but the star part of the
Fairy Princess was written for a big girl about to leave school. Iris told
me she was always kind and encouraging to the young ones. Her name
was June Duprez. Her father was an impresario of some kind, and
later on managed to get his daughter, who was exceedingly pretty, the
star part of the Persian Princess in a wartime Korda film called *The
Thief of Baghdad*.

Done in sumptuous Technicolor, *The Thief of Baghdad* was deserv-
edly successful, and June Duprez was absolutely sweet as well as
beautiful. She couldn't act for toffee, however much of a success she
may have been with Iris and the rabbits, and I believe her subsequent
career in films faded painlessly out. This film had a lot of stunning
special effects – the genie emerging out of his bottle in a great black
cloud, and the 'child' star Sabu, known as the 'Elephant Boy', riding
on his magic carpet over spectacular Arabian mountains and ravines,
no doubt borrowed from some Californian footage the studio happened to have around. It was all shot in Pinewood, during the war.

I remember the shock of coming out of the small cinema where
these wonders had taken place into the grey winter afternoon in
Gerrards Cross; and in my memory now June Duprez and the young
Caliph and the villainous Vizier Conrad Veidt, with his green eyes and
sinister German accent, have somehow got mixed up with Iris's rabbit
play, her early morning wow-wer-wows, and the haunting little jingle
from *Petrushka*, which Stravinsky first heard on the barrel organ.
Wow-wows had in any case been our recognition signal from early
days. If I came back to the house and couldn't find Iris at once I used

to give a wow or two and hear a distant wow-wow in response, and more of them as we came closer to each other.

Even today my pulses would quicken a little at the sight of June Duprez in that film. In her elocution school accent she repelled the advances of Conrad Veidt until he got the young Caliph in his power and threatened to blind him and throw him in a dungeon. Then: 'Take me in your arms,' she told the villainous Veidt with icy disdain, sounding as if she had just come back from helping with the school treat at whatever academy young Sabu attended. I forget how she was rescued, but I still vividly recall the moment earlier on when the young Caliph climbed a tree overlooking the harem garden in order to see her. Sitting with her ladies at the edge of a pool – fully clothed of course – she sees his face reflected in the water, and hears his disembodied voice swearing that he loves her.

'Now that you have found me, O genie of the pool, will you love me to the end of the world?'

I sometimes used to imitate that speech for Iris when we spoke of her early schooldays, and she always shed a tear or two, and told me how nice June had been to the little ones, which I could well believe, and how the school had idolised her. Probably some of the mistresses too, I should imagine.

I once suggested to Iris that we write together an academic version of the rabbit play, with a chorus of inebriated dons chanting:

> We don't care for the thinky girls
> What we want are slinky girls,
> Minky girls, kinky girls, winky girls,
> And most of all the drinky girls …

So far as I can recall no more was done, but we used to chant something like that in the car sometimes. It became a part of our mythology.

So did two other songs we used to play: 'Yellow Bird' and 'Yellow Submarine'.

'Yellow bird, you seem all alone like me,' Iris would hum, looking at me with a fond look, which seemed to imply that I was never to be alone like the bird; even though, as we both knew, being married was the best possible way of being alone. I used to tell Iris that I was annoyed with the lyrics of 'Yellow Submarine'. The chorus should have taken up the words of the grizzled mariner who supposedly tells them about his life in the land of submarines. 'We all lived in a yellow submarine' it should go, I thought: not 'live' in a yellow submarine. I preferred the notion of past dangers and wartime patrols, to the distasteful idea of a contemporary rave, in which the old salt's tale is forgotten. To the young, in any case, the song itself must now seem antediluvian.

If I got too pedantic about such things Iris sometimes said 'Woof Woof', like a dog, impatient for its owner to stop talking and take it for a walk. She herself was a stickler for accuracy in her novels, and she enjoyed any procedure that was intent on getting things right. A Canadian friend of hers, a philosopher who had taught at a military academy, once fascinated her by explaining how important it was to get right the exact proportions of the new Canadian flag: the maple leaf just the right size and in the middle of the white centre section, the red borders neither too big nor too small. I had a fondness for flags myself. Iris bought me a handbook called *Flags of the World* or some such title, and while she was away with a delegation in China for three or four weeks – the longest time we were ever separated – I made some Valentine flags for her return. By coincidence she came back on 14 February. The flags were of Catland, as we called our own imaginary country.

Today I found the big card, quite unexpectedly; it was preserved carefully at the bottom of a cluttered drawer in Iris's study, or rather the room upstairs where she wrote. 'Study' sounds like an organised methodical place, and the room where Iris wrote was anything but that. The quantity of papers and books and sea-stones and shoes and bits of clothing, to say nothing of less identifiable rubbish, is so great that I have done nothing about it; I didn't want even to go in there. This morning I tried just to drift in absently, determined not to make it seem like an act of the will, but I realised as I poked about that I had been almost frightened to go in before.

Was this because of the concentration of now derelict or indefinable things that had once meant something to Iris, even if briefly? Of the scraps of letters, some half-finished, or hardly begun, I felt an almost superstitious horror. But I was glad anyway to find my valentine for that year, '*The Flags of Old Catland*', although it had faded almost out of recognition. My crimson and dark-blue designs had turned pink and grey over the years; the chalks, or whatever it was I had used, had certainly not been colour-fast.

But the one I remembered having been proudest of and had given pride of place in the centre of the design, 'The Banner of the Fighting Mouse', still looked bold and black. The mouse's belligerent whiskers, done in Indian ink, were still as spruce and sharply defined as they were all those years ago, when 'How's that catmouse?' was a greeting between us.

The Chinese expedition, I recall, was quite a grand one, headed by Richard Attenborough. Iris was one of the distinguished female delegates, presumably representing art and letters. They had an audience with Deng Xiaoping, the Party boss and head of the government. They travelled mostly by train, staying in vast and gloomy hotels. In one of these a party of Rolls-Royce engineers was rumoured to be billeted. Iris and a couple of others set out to walk the long corridors in search of these fellow-countrymen, and Iris made the ingenious suggestion that they should chant 'Rule Britannia' as they went. It worked like a charm. Doors flew open and lonely engineers swarmed out, eager in their solitude to meet up with compatriots.

On another occasion Iris found herself talking in a general way to some Chinese peasant women. As they all relaxed – audiences always did that with Iris – the women began to ply the interpreter with questions. The interpreter, an efficient and sophisticated lady from Beijing who was minding the delegation, looked rather embarrassed. Iris made enquiry.

'Well, you must excuse please, Miss Murdoch. They are simple people, and they are asking if Western women are the same as Chinese, or different.'

The interpreter made matters clear by sketching in the air below her waist with a delicate forefinger. Iris assured the peasant ladies, rather to their disappointment she felt, that those arrangements were the same throughout the world, at least so far as she knew. The story grew in the telling. Another female member of the delegation swore that Iris had promptly dropped her skirt and pants and given a practical demonstration, which met with hearty acclaim. That seems most unlikely; Iris said nothing about it to me. She had a great deal of natural modesty, and in spite of their curiosity I imagine that the Chinese ladies would have understood that.

*

Do all widows and widowers go through a time of hearing the voice? Or perhaps it's more a question of listening involuntarily to what the voice suggests? Inflections, pet words, scraps of song? At moments the 'Yellow Submarine'; then the little theme from *Petrushka*. That is the most insistent of all. Iris always took it up if I started to try to hum it and we made a hash of it together. We loved trying to put that last 'wow' in the right place.

I began to hum it this morning, almost masochistically, as I sought a footing amongst all the varied junk that covered the floor of Iris's room. And as I hummed, an unfamiliar name popped into my head. Maud Bigge. Who was she and where had she come from? Was there an association with *Petrushka*? Yes, indeed there was. I hummed again, hearing Iris hum too, and the title came to me. *My Secret London*, by Maud Bigge. She must have been a journalist of the Twenties or Thirties, who probably wrote for the *Evening News* or *Standard*. She must have assembled her pieces into a book; now I remember its colour, and that it was published by Methuen.

I was six or seven. My godmother had given it to my mother as a birthday present. I was bidden to write a birthday greeting on the flyleaf, which I accomplished laboriously in pencil.

I doubt if my mother ever read the book. I rediscovered it, tucked away on the shelf in a corner of her bedroom, when I was just about to go back to boarding school. It was going to be my second term and I felt apprehensive and miserable. On an impulse I asked if I could take the book back with me; anything about London could only be comforting. My mother let me do that, and I was not wrong: the book *was* cheering.

Hard now to imagine why. The unpretentious, quietly amusing, sometimes sentimental little book became a part of my imaginative life. And *Petrushka* came into it. Miss Bigge (or Mrs, but I still like to think Miss) had attended a performance of Stravinsky's ballet in London, and the clown Petrushka had touched her heart. She wrote a whole piece about him.

I remember finding the book years and years ago – it must have been some time after we got married. But then I felt not the smallest revival of interest in it and so it dropped out of sight again. Now I've spent two days searching for it – all over the house. Quite uselessly. It has gone back into the shadowy old London of those days, together with its unknown author.

Could she be still alive? Hardly. But it feels as if both of us are in the widowed state. Maud Bigge and her book have disappeared as definitively as Iris has. But Iris's books live on. I hope Maud Bigge's do too, somewhere, and are still read by some old lady or gent like myself, who has taken them from the bookcase in the same fit of nostalgia.

I imagine Maud Bigge as a jolly, spirited young woman, with dark hair and a decisive manner. The sort of woman whom a boy at the age of twelve or so would get on with. And I was touched by her tenderness for poor Petrushka, whom I had never heard of before.

Iris had never heard of Maud Bigge, nor seen the book, and her interest in *Petrushka* was limited to the little hum which pleased her even after she became ill, because we used to hum it together. In happier times she loved more robust affairs, like the Irish songs of Percy French, who wrote 'Abdul the Bul-Bul Emir' and sold it to a

Dublin publisher for five shillings. Had he retained the copyright it would have made him many thousands of pounds.

Iris also knew all the words of 'The Old Orange Flute' and in the days before she was ill would sing it with great *brio*.

> In the midst of the flames there was heard a great noise,
> 'Twas the old flute still playing 'The Protestant Boys'.

'The Protestant Boys' was originally sung to the tune of 'Liliburlero', the defiantly ironic little ditty with words invented by Protestant singers to suggest the sort of gibberish that they thought of the native Irish as speaking. The BBC World Service has now adopted it for a signature tune. Probably the tune was already old when Purcell used it in a harmonious suite. A few politically-correct PR men suggested to the Corporation that the Irish might not like it, but one hopes the Irish have more sense than that, as well more sense of humour.

I sometimes teased Iris about her staunch Irish Protestantism, whereupon she would purse up her lips and smile forgivingly, implying that although I might know something of history I none the less knew nothing about Ireland. That may well be true; but I used to remind her of my Irish grandfather, name of Heenan, a promising engineer who came over to England to seek his fortune. He found it, and ceased to be an Irishman; or at least he preferred to forget that he was one. That was common enough at the time, but things today are very different. The English now fall over themselves to claim Irish or Scottish ancestry; but it is an odd fact that no Scot or Irishman has ever been known to claim that he is partly English.

CHAPTER SEVEN

Canary

There was a time, after Iris died, when things got better, or at least different. My fortnight with our old friend Audi in the Canary Isles.

Although seldom able to be in England, Audi was immensely helpful to Iris when she came. Iris loved her. In the days when she was well they had a very special relationship. Friends used to say, what do they talk about all the time?

Audi has been many years a widow, a veteran in the trade. She said, and says, nothing about it, but I know now how much and how continually she misses her husband. We were friends for so long, the four of us: Borys and Audi and Iris and I. Every summer we did a bit of travelling together, and we often stayed in the little house they had built on the island of Lanzarote, partly on account of Audi's severe asthma. The climate relieved it.

Their house was right in the middle of the rocky volcanic island, far away from the crowded beaches. In the days when they built the house, the beaches were not crowded. There was no telephone, uncertain electricity. Very little water, for rain hardly ever fell. Very few people. Now the island has been 'developed'. With the usual results.

The island grows on me none the less. I detested it at first. The Sunset Strips along the beaches, full of discos and Irish pubs and Viking wine bars. They look like all such places, only even more so. But once we are away from the coast all this disappears; and although the island is not much more than fifty miles long there is a good deal of quiet country inland. Tourist buses go to the Fire Mountain, a mass of coagulated lava with one or two small bits of permanent volcanic activity; but the real character of the place is not in these outlandish and comparatively recent manifestations of subterranean inferno. It is in the round hills that swell up from the tawny landscape in conical, almost pyramidal shapes, with a strange and slightly uncanny lightness and grace about them. They are smooth and bare, untrodden by tourists, and in the evening their silhouettes cut the lucid sky into shapes that can look both razor-sharp and voluptuously tender. The strange world they come from, silent and distant and long extinct, has nothing to do with the ever-growing pullulation on the island shores. Nor with the reddish contortions of the Fire Mountain, that volcanic parvenu whose ungainly bulk, like a noisome and decaying monster, reveals at a distance the tourist buses on their perpetual scenic round, crawling over it like maggots.

This unquiet effect is even presented by the low island cliffs, the only alternative to the beaches on the sheltered eastern coast line. At a distance they relieve the eye by seeming bare and unpopulated, but as you come closer you see that every fissure and cranny contains human figures. Heavy-looking topless girls bask awkwardly in each sunny niche, while their German boyfriends cling and crawl indefatigably, vying with each other to get to the cliff top, or in finding ways down to the obedient sea at its base.

Lanzarote is not an island to give you any illusion of wide open spaces. It is claustrophobic in the extreme. But although the flat white houses between and at the foot of the hills are constantly multiplying, as if they too were maggots, there are still inland corners by the conical hills where there is no movement, no sound but the steady trade-wind blowing and the occasional call of a hoopoe. When flying, those bizarre birds resemble giant moths, so sharply contrasted on their wings is the patterning of black and white and cinnamon brown.

Audi's house is in one of these still secluded places. It is white, like all the island houses, with a lot of bougainvillaea in striking shades of mauve, orange and maroon and a garden of pepper trees and little palms like pineapples, growing in semi-circular compounds made of the black lava stone. To give it further protection from the wind, each tree stands in a shallow dimple scooped out of the black sand-like *picon*, velvety-looking ground-up lava which holds the strong fall of dew. There is usually no rain at all on the island, and this soft dimple of *picon* helps the trees survive.

It keeps vines going too. In the remote parts of the island there are whole slopes and acres of such dimpled depressions, each with a few wizened shoots at the bottom. They run up the sides of the smooth hills, making them sleek and black to a certain height instead of the strange golden-brown which is always changing under cloud shadows in the pure, brilliant light. The wine produced in this way is expensive, naturally enough, and not specially good, although it is drunk by some of the residents and a few tourists, out of a sense of loyalty.

The English residents, of whom there are not very many, rarely speak more than a few words of Spanish, and see comparatively little of one another. Nor do they hob-nob with the natives or with the tourists. It is a bit of a mystery what residents find to do, since they do not engage in tourist activities. They probably watch TV and videos, just as they would at home.

One resident I met said confidentially as we drank some of the local wine: 'You know, there are people who come to Lanzarote and never leave again.' He paused for a moment's rumination and added: 'Others leave at once.'

But the place does grow on one, no doubt about that. The coast of Africa is not far off; the flat-roofed houses with thick white walls that look as if they were made of adobe have a Moorish look. Audi's has no staircase, but it is built on different levels and the roomy interior is paved with Spanish and Italian tiles, which the warm wind sprinkles with black *picon* from the garden. Audi is often out there, watering the Teresita and Plumbago flowers on the terrace, or grooming the soft cup-shaped black hollows in which lemon and olive and fig-trees do their best to grow.

In the evenings Audi played Patience and I sat reading, looking up from time to time to ask her something. In the daytime it was a relief not to have to do anything much except go to the shop. The time passed very well.

Iris used to love it here, and Audi used to drive us to the sea so that Iris could swim. Afterwards she took us to a small fishy place where she and I sometimes had a scarce local delicacy unknown to the tourists; Iris, who distrusted fish, stuck to an egg and salad. Our strange creatures, known as *clacas*, came from a part of the rough western coast facing the Atlantic, where the shoreline is a mass of jagged black lava boulders left over from the last eruption. The locals lower themselves on ropes to prise off these giant barnacles, which are then boiled in sea-water. To eat them you fish them out one at a time with a bit of wire; the scrap tastes like very tender lobster. You then drink the warm liquid from the aperture, a delicate marine soup which might have been used to baptise Venus.

Audi knew all the quieter places where it was possible to bathe, including one frequented by brown and naked German grandmothers. They seemed to resent our clothed state, but smiled forgivingly at us none the less. As her illness increased Iris became afraid to bathe, and Audi used to take her into the shower at home. She loved that.

*

Evening on the island is the best time. Although the Canaries are well above the tropics, night here comes on at a run.

> The sun's rim dips, the stars rush out,
> With one stride comes the dark ...

So Coleridge put it in *The Ancient Mariner*. Malta was the furthest south he went, and that was long after he had written the poem. He was secretary to the governor, Sir Alexander Ball, who had been one of Nelson's captains at the great Nile victory. How on earth did Coleridge get the job? How did he hold it down? Possibly through being such a wonderful talker – people really loved conversation in those days.

From Richard Holmes's biography I remember a touching detail. Because of his opium habit Coleridge suffered so severely from constipation on the way out to Malta that the fleet surgeon had to be rowed across to put things right. But once arrived the poet was the life and soul of the local dinner parties. Perhaps he was really just employed to talk, and to keep the English garrison entertained and amused. He seems to have been no use as a secretary, but Sir Alexander tolerated him manfully. How would he have got on in Lanzarote today? Not too well probably.

And yet he would so much have enjoyed the dinner party we had during my holiday. Prawns, *osso bucco*, lots of red wine. (From the mainland, although we loyally drank some Lanzarote white wine as an aperitif.) Dinner ended in laughter and good cheer, which would have pleased Coleridge and his contemporaries.

An English guest told what he said was not an old Spanish joke but a true story he had heard from the local barman, who was a character. A man once asked him for a drink compounded of kümmel, aniseed, vermouth, crème de menthe, grappa and a few other things. He drank and made a face.

'Excuse me, sir,' said the barman, 'but do you really like that stuff?'

'No,' the man said. 'I drink it because it reminds me of the taste of a woman.'

The barman, intrigued, asked to try the drink. He tasted it and shook his head. '*Ne parecido*,' he said. 'Not a bit like.'

Laughter anyway, especially from the ladies, who must feel it important not to seem stuffy or feminist. I suspected the point of the story had been watered down a bit; but many Spanish sayings have an enigmatic air about them.

'With St Joseph, a beard, without, the Virgin Mary.'

What can that one mean? It teases you with a suggestion of something louche but obscure. You must be in the know to get the point, if indeed there is one. Coleridge might have enjoyed the barman's story, but not have told it in mixed company? His parson father, who sounds rather like him, was once keeping the table in a roar when he glanced down and saw his shirt front was coming out. He tucked it in and went on talking, but in a minute or two he noticed it was out again. This went on until the ladies got up to leave, when it was found that his neighbour had the long white skirt of her dress securely tucked into the parson's waistband.

141

I remember and tell the story, which has its moment of amusement. A tall Norwegian with a charming voice begins without preamble on a Scandinavian joke, the equivalent of our laborious old ones about the Englishman, Irishman and Scotsman. A Norwegian, a Swede and a Dane, revolutionaries in South America, are caught by government troops. 'Alas, gentlemen,' says the general, 'we shall have to shoot you, but you shall each have a last wish.' The Dane chooses a steak, a bottle of wine and a cigar. The Norwegian wants to make a speech. That leaves the Swede, who says would they mind shooting him before the Norwegian makes his speech.

Much laughter and applause. Audi has told me of her countrymen's fondness for making after-dinner speeches; and this story, needless to say, was invented by a Norwegian.

The birds of Lanzarote give great pleasure, although there are not many of them. Just before dusk falls the hoopoes sometimes come, flittering among the diminutive pepper and acacia trees. Striped alternately in black and white, their moth-like wings show up boldly against their drab body plumage. On the ground they are almost invisible, but the agitated movement of wings shows where the little group are until they settle among the trees and disappear. They are small birds, hardly bigger than the thrush, and they grow in size and presence when they spread their great crests, rufous colour tipped with black and white, like the head-dress of an Indian chief. They nest among the low stone walls, built of black lava and left full of holes so that the wind won't blow them down.

As we watched the hoopoes through the window, settling themselves for the night, they reminded me of a fussy group of maiden ladies quarrelling politely over the rooms allocated them in a crowded hotel. Their profile, as the birdwatchers say, suggests a kind of faded Edwardian femininity.

Another bird that has almost disappeared in England used to visit round the house in Lanzarote – the Great Grey Shrike. Despite his majestic name and his very definite masculinity compared to the feminine hoopoes, he was not very big either. But he was very assertive. He perched at the top of a tall cactus or euphorbia, keeping watch for the lizards and beetles he preyed upon, and uttering a harsh note, almost a bark, like an irate colonel. His Latin name is *excubitor*, the sentinel: literally, I suppose, the one who has to stay out of bed. In Spanish he is 'Alcairon', which Audi thought had a Moorish sound; it may mean the same sort of thing in that language. Candellaria, Audi's cleaning lady, told us a rhyme in the local Canary dialect.

> *Alcairon, Alcairon, que noticias traes?*
> *Si es para mi*
> *Deja lo aqui*
> *Si es para otro que te vaya.*

'Shrike, shrike, what news do you bring? If it's for me leave it here, if it's for someone else, go away.'

Audi was very knowledgeable about local and many other matters. Useless but fascinating information has always cheered me up, and here at last I found my old appetite for it returning. But only for things that were safely and entrancingly in the past, a point even explaining my fondness for the hoopoes, with their air not only of bizarre and gigantic moths but of string and calico aircraft from the dawn of human flight. All my 'aeroplane books', as Iris called them, were about obsolete aircraft, ships and weaponry, never the modern ones.

*

Bereavement too can seem old-fashioned and obsolete; perhaps I embraced the idea of it for that reason. The Victorians were good at it, so to speak – the period seems to have been full of widows and widowers in becoming black clothes. But at the same time as I feel nostalgia and affection for the bereaved who are past and gone, I feel an equal urge to analyse the state of bereavement, in the modern clinical manner.

Shall I be the shrink or the patient? It hardly matters. The canny shrink (he sounds like the shrike – does he too bring news?) obviously perceives this indifference; and makes a note of it? But I'm tired of the shrink already. His eyes have noted a loss of weight, otherwise no marked physical deterioration.

'Bereaved persons have a tendency to idealise the dead loved one,' he says blandly.

Do I do that? I wouldn't have thought so. True, I found myself thinking the other day, in the context of our mutual acquaintance, that I had never heard Iris speak ill of anyone, or say anything sharp about any of our friends. But that wasn't idealising her. It was no more than the truth. And it sometimes irritated me when I would have liked a good malicious gossip about some tiresome acquaintance recently endured. Iris had her own brand of wholly private political correctness. She didn't disapprove of gossip and backbiting; she just never indulged in them herself.

So I don't idealise her. I am remembering her as she was, as she was for me.

But the bereaved soon discover that there are two sorts of memories involved. There are deliberate memories, of what we did and what we said. I summon her up: walking, talking, sitting down, washing the dishes. But after a few moments of deliberate recollection this person loses outline; she becomes not just shadowy, but unreal. She will not stay in place. I cannot even be sure she is the right person.

Then sometimes, without warning, involuntary memory can still ambush me, like a ruffian on the stairs. That is authentic, the real thing, staying for no more than a second or two. There she is suddenly, the vision that makes me cry with grief just because it is so true; because I have not created it. It came in Lanzarote, just as it had done at home. Or I opened a door, in either place, and heard the real Iris say 'Wow Wow' as she looked up with a smile from her work.

On our last trip together to Lanzarote, Iris and I saw again the one or two places which had begun to have their own sort of private importance for us. We looked at each other with a smile when Audi drove us past viewpoints with which we had developed our own brand of intimacy. A white speck on the brown flank of a conical mountain had intrigued us, visible at a great distance in the glass-clear air. It turned out to be a rusty white car panel, abandoned – heaven knows why – far up, and far from any road.

Then there was a kind of house beside the huge lava rocks on the wild western shore, a small rectangular hotel, abandoned and derelict, like a building in the background of a Magritte painting. We were fascinated by it; it was the only really lonely place on the island. The Swedish owner had hoped to make an artificial beach among the sea-buffeted rocks, but it came to nothing. Audi said that the locals had stripped and carried off all the fittings, including windows and doors. I spotted the white car panel again, but I no longer felt the fascination of old when we passed by the derelict hotel the other evening. This again seemed the index of a more general lack of interest in things.

I felt half tempted to ask Audi if she had felt the same sort of lack of interest after Borys died, but I said nothing, which seemed easier. I knew how much she had missed him, still missed him. In terms of missingness I had a long way to go before I was up to her level.

*

Back in Oxford, alone in my house, I found that the freedom and the solitude, which I had once wistfully supposed to be the positive side of bereavement, still showed no signs of arriving. Doing things that should have occupied and consoled me made me feel as miserably anxious as poor Iris had been when she first began to suffer from Alzheimer's. I felt busier and more bothered than ever, and the distractions that are supposed to keep the mind off things seemed quite unable to do that job.

And I missed kind, learned Audi, who knows about the birds of the Canaries, and the volcanoes and the cochineal plantations, and about sailing and sailing-ships and the discovery of longitude. She even knows all about the Guanchos, the mysterious people who lived on the Canary Islands before the Spaniards arrived. They must have originally come over from Africa. Having arrived, they or their descendants forgot how to use or to make boats, so that they could not even move from one island to another. Guanchos in Lanzarote lived mostly in remote caves at the northern end of the island.

Margot and Mella have passed like a dream, but I keep remembering those earlier days in Lanzarote.

Iris and Audi used to meet on their own in London and chatter happily away together over lunch or supper. Iris had a natural seriousness and rarely laughed, but she would go into fits of laughter over things that Borys and Audi said and told her.

I say that now, and I know it's true; and yet I can't really remember. Was Iris fond of laughing and joking? She must have been, but it doesn't sound right, like so many of the things that one says about people after they have gone, or indeed before they go. Personality never really survives reminiscence and discussion. But voices do.

Watching Audi playing her game and occasionally making some remark, I used to concentrate my own attention on the theme of Forgotten Wars. That helped to stop the voices coming back into my head, both the one I had heard and the one I could not hear.

I was reading a novel recommended by Audi called *The Blue Afternoon*, by William Boyd. It is set in the Philippines during the Spanish-American war – 1900 or so – when many Filipinos were all for independence, and the Americans had decided in paternal fashion that they weren't yet ready for it. A gripping love story about a surgeon and an officer's wife vividly suggests the background of the place and period. The war began in 1899 after the liberation of the Philippines from Spanish rule, raged until 1903, and dragged on in some of the islands until 1914. It was full of incidents which make the My Lai massacre in Vietnam seem mild and insignificant.

I remember reading in Louis Untermeyer's long outdated anthology a few high-minded and suitably agonised poems which American women poets wrote about this wicked war – the equivalent, in those days, of campus protests and peace marches against Vietnam.

Shame-faced victors and gallant losers are alike forgotten today. Many American soldiers, as in Vietnam, came from the Southern states, and some must have recalled their own struggle against the Union, not much more than thirty years before. The difference is that this Philippines war is forgotten, by common consent as it seems, while the Civil War is consecrated for ever in American folk memory and legend.

Rudyard Kipling was highly gratified by the Philippines conflict and wrote a poem about it, which Americans thought in the worst of taste.

> Take up the White Man's burden,
> The savage wars of peace ...

That brilliant bit of self-congratulation, self-exculpation too, has certainly survived. It was only a short time since our own Zulu War and the war in the Sudan against the Mahdi, both accompanied by the usual massacres. The British Army was keeping busy, and was about to embark on a conflict with the Boers – a 'Sahibs' War', as Kipling called it – but more significant for him was the heartening spectacle of the Land of the Free joining the British Empire in its perennial police actions against primitive people, who had to be civilised, one way or another.

All forgotten now. Except by the historians, a novelist maybe, and a few politicians as and if it suits them. For them – for me too – it has all become part of the comfort of history. Wordsworth himself wrote a memorable line or two when he spoke of 'old unhappy far-off things and battles long ago'. But he was wrong. They are not really unhappy. Time always has enough distance to cheer us up. The great healer. But only across the centuries, not in terms of one year.

*

And the first year of bereavement is probably the best. Not the worst. That is a thought to make me feel uneasy, but nothing can be done about it. That is why I cling as tightly as I can to thoughts about the past. Wars, battles, things that were: and things that might have been. The wars of Hannibal and Belisarius. The wars of Jenkins's Ear and the Spanish succession ...

Memories, day-dreams, associations. All useful for the comfort process. Reading Boyd's excellent novel reminded me of the museum at Tromsø in North Norway. I asked Audi, who is Norwegian after all, if she'd ever been there, but she hadn't. I remember it well. Iris and I were giving a talk there once, arranged by the British Council and the local university. I don't remember much of what we said, or whom we met, but I vividly remember the little museum, which was devoted to the history of Norwegian settlers in Spitzbergen and the Arctic. It had life-size models of Arctic huts in the snow, and dummies dressed in white furs. I was especially fascinated by the model of a polar bear trap. These bears were a deadly danger to the settlers, who often had to spend a solitary winter in a snowhouse. To kill the bear you arranged a large piece of seal meat on a stand outside a hide. Inside it was a rifle, carefully aligned on a point just above the bait, from which a string was attached to its trigger. When the bear seized the bait it pulled the string and the rifle went off. With luck all round, instant end of bear.

I recognised the rifle – a genuine article – in the museum tableau. After the war I was in Norway with the army, and I saw a good deal of the celebrated Krag-Jörgensen rifle, still used then by Norwegian troops, as it had been used by the American army more than forty years before in the Philippines. It was a simple gun, but it had earned an international reputation for its phenomenal accuracy at long range. The Norwegians were justly proud of this weapon – even Audi knew about it – and it was often mentioned in *The Blue Afternoon*.

Thinking about the Krag-Jörgensen – known to American soldiers simply as 'the Krag' – and watching Audi tranquilly playing out her Patience, seemed like a phantom replay of Iris and myself. Years ago, when we lived at Steeple Aston, Iris would soon be asleep when we went to bed, tired with a long day's writing, and I would lie browsing in one of my 'aeroplane' books. For a surprise present she once ordered a series called the *Phoebus History of Two World Wars*, which featured not so much the wars themselves as the weapons employed in them. I used to browse over machine-guns, tanks and Messerschmidts, while Iris slept tranquilly beside me. Very often she would wake up in the small hours and pad round to my side of the bed to turn off the light and remove my spectacles. The Krag-Jörgensen –

a resounding name like my other favourites – had revived the memory, together with Audi's quiet concentration while I dreamily read my book.

Two people, each doing their own separate thing. It is a situation that is always happening. In offices or in families. No doubt also in ships and aeroplanes. The steersman motionless at the wheel, while the officer of the watch paces calmly up and down the bridge. Or is all that obsolete? But the idea of a pair, in the communion of a mutual non-awareness – that has its own significance. Widows and widowers must often brood about it, as they find out what it once meant to them.

I dreamed over that *Phoebus History* as I used to dream, between the wars at the age of eight, over the historical drawings in Warne's *Pictorial Knowledge*. Pictures of Hannibal and his men, sword in hand, gazing down from the Alps; Napoleon at the battle of Lodi, or on the island of St Helena … I don't think I would have enjoyed the aeroplane books as I did without the presence of those old memories, and of Iris asleep beside me.

For the bereaved the worst – or the best? – moment is remembering those times together, each unconscious of the other. But when Iris was ill with Alzheimer's, I only enjoyed my day-dreaming when we were together, on one of our endless little walks round the block, or when I lay beside her in bed and she was gently snoring, released for a few hours from the perpetual restlessness and anxiety which compelled her to wander round the house in the small hours, collecting her oddments together.

During those days and nights, when Iris was ill, and in a weird way all the more companionable for being ill, my usual dreams were narrative fantasies, long-running soap operas of imagined lives, which I conjured into existence and changed at will. The most persistent, as venerable as one of Iris's comic strips in the *Evening Standard*, concerned the Big Woman of Gerrards Cross.

The Big Woman was just that: a lady of immense height and size, who lived in a nice house left her by her father, whom she had looked after devotedly for many years. She lived alone now, and was much involved in good works and church activities.

My own relations with the Big Woman were equivocal and varied a good deal. Sometimes I preferred, as it were, not to know her but only to think about her. Sometimes, in my imagination, the Big Woman had a female friend staying with her, and the Vicar had brought them both along to a party. I can hear his breezy tones, 'apologising' to the hostess, in the way the clergy do, for having 'inflicted' two extra guests on her. 'But Miss' (I fail to catch her name) 'is such a blessing, such a help to me. A real pillar of strength, a *tower*, you know.' His unctuous tones waver for a moment, as if it has just occurred to him, as it must have done to everyone else within earshot, that he has chosen his metaphors not quite fortunately, in view of the lady's remarkable height and size. She and her friend look predictably embarrassed; not by his words but by the fact that they are at the party at all.

Filled, in my day-dream, with sudden inspiration I go boldly up to the Big Woman. I smile up at her – my very best smile. Warm, friendly, reassuring, conveying a certainty that she and I understand one another, are two of a kind. Her own smile, remote as a lighthouse but not distant, beams down gratefully upon me.

The scenario had many variations. Sometimes it stopped altogether, and then restarted itself at some other point in the saga. It was important that nothing very dramatic should happen. No love, no kisses. The Big Woman was not exactly intended for that sort of thing. Our relationship is secret, innocent ... We understand each other wholly, and the feeling of unspoken intimacy between us is at times almost overpowering ...

Meanwhile I would be walking hand in hand with Iris, round the block. Often she would drop my hand and fumble on the pavement for a bit of silver paper that had caught her eye, a plastic top, even a cigarette end. She examined them carefully. Did they hold some message for her? Hard not to imagine that these fragments were becoming the properties of some scene with which she was inwardly preoccupied.

It soothed me to believe what I felt, even knew, to be unbelievable: that Iris still had an inner life to match my own. *Far* greater than my own. Could that brain, once creating so many fantasies, stories, situations for novels which had become true masterpieces – could that brain really be closing down completely, paralysed and trapped in the lesions and irregular plaques that had developed on its unseen but mysterious, once symmetric, surface? I wanted to believe that just as we had once lain in bed together – me reading my aeroplane books, she tranquilly asleep, or me pottering in the house and garden, doing some absorbing little thing, and she waving from the window and continuing her writing – so, even at the worst, some unknown harmonious mutual activity between us must be still going on.

*

Those moments in the street came back to me as I turned the page of the book, and looked up at Audi, quietly working away at her Patience. Audi and the Krag-Jörgensen rifle, and the Big Woman of Gerrards Cross – all mixed up …

This must be all part of being a widower. I used to be good at marshalling thoughts and sentences, getting what I wanted to say into some kind of order. Now I slip and slide. From one thing to another, without knowing whether it's memory, fantasy, something old or something new. Typical bereavement syndrome?

I realise, or think I realise, what is happening. Something inside is putting things together, laboriously stitching a presence together out of an absence. A presence involves two people. Separate from one another, unconscious of each other's presence, and, because unconscious, all the closer together. Closer and closer apart.

That phrase used to comfort me a great deal because I only read it, and the poem of which it's a part, after Iris had started to be ill with Alzheimer's. It described so well our former relationship, of which I only became aware after the illness had virtually taken it away. The poem is by A.D. Hope, a mysterious Australian about whom I know nothing at all except for that line from one of his poems.

When Iris was ill we could still communicate – we seemed to do so just as much as ever – but those moments of tranquil apartness, togetherness in apartness, were no longer there. I was no longer reading my aeroplane books while Iris was writing quietly away, or waving to me from the window with one hand while writing with the other. But as I dreamily watched Audi playing Patience, and then looked at my book, the same pattern seemed to be forming again.

But, like all patterns, it was different. Iris didn't read novels. Audi does, and she had read this one, which was why I was reading it; and every so often I asked her something about it. With her eyes on the Patience cards she replied, sensibly but abstractedly, and I forgot what she had said and dipped back quietly into the book again. There is a lot about obscure illnesses in the book, for its hero is a surgeon; and Audi, who has had severe asthma attacks all her life, and allergies since she was born, knows a very great deal about illnesses and about being ill.

When staying with her I really enjoyed reading books – new and old, familiar and unfamiliar – for the first time since Iris became ill. In addition to *The Blue Afternoon* I found Audi's paperback of *A Handful of Dust* and re-read it, for the third or fourth time, with even greater enjoyment. It is the sort of masterpiece which, like Jane Austen's, presents a subtly different picture and a different emphasis with each re-reading. I had always had the impression before that the characters were too much made use of by the author, who had his own decidedly unartistic axe to grind: namely, revenge against the wife who had left him, and the man she had gone off with. Through the imaginary characters, Brenda Last and John Beaver, Waugh portrayed these two real persons, at least for his own satisfaction, in as disagreeable a light as possible.

But however familiar one may be with Evelyn Waugh's life and the unlucky history of his first marriage, the art of the novel wins hands down. I used to think that the reaction of Brenda Last to the news of her little boy's death in the hunting field was dramatically effective but psychologically implausible. Now it seems to me all of a part with Waugh's understanding of the social world he both inhabited and created. Brenda is not a monster of cold egoism; she has the extreme inner carelessness involuntarily nurtured by her set, and by the society she moves in. Life as she finds herself living it, in an ugly great country house with her adoring husband and her little boy, is simply not real to her, not to be cared about. She is not just bored; she has no sense of life's true necessities, their promise and design. John Beaver, the vulgar nonentity whom no one else wants, represents for her a reality she can seize and own for herself, a reality that brings her her first awareness of love. By throwing herself at him she can make both him and herself real. Almost 'caring', in fact.

I very much sympathise with Brenda. In fact, since Iris died I have been feeling rather like a Brenda myself, but a Brenda whose sense of reality has gone, rather than one who has suddenly found it. Widowers are not necessarily monsters of egoism, but perhaps they may suddenly find in themselves that same inner carelessness. I feel I am doing a Brenda all the time. I have lost my Beaver. I have suffered bereavement.

John Beaver, as drawn by Waugh, is a perfect mate for Brenda. Neither have anything inside them. I feel an affinity now with him too. No more inner life, no more Belial thoughts that wander through eternity …

The life of the couple is supplied entirely by what they can get from society. But Brenda unexpectedly finds herself capable of love, although she does not recognise it as such, while Beaver sees her only as a means of getting on in smart society. In the eyes of their friends they both become interesting because of the improbability of their relationship, and both are gratified by the fact. A lesser artist might have portrayed Beaver as a mother's boy, but Waugh's Beaver is not even that. He uses his mother so far as he can, just as he uses any contact that will aid his social advancement. This is the man for whom Brenda bursts out 'Oh, thank God,' when she finds that it is not he who has been killed in an aeroplane accident, as she feared, but only her little boy in the hunting field.

Brenda cannot bear the thought of the one *real* object that is her own being taken from her; Beaver is merely gratified that society gossip is so enthralled by their unlikely and unexpected walk-out. There must be more to him, society concludes, than meets the eye. But there is nothing, nothing at all, and Brenda loves him just for that. With him at last there is no need for her to deceive, or to play a part.

Would Brenda have married her Beaver if he would have had her? Would the marriage have lasted if he had? Hard to say. Perhaps it would, in its own way; she might have stuck to him like a leech. Her own. But that's outside the particular heart of this novel, the circle in which, as Henry James said, the relations of life which end nowhere must happily *appear* to do so. Brenda ends up marrying Jock, her husband's oldest friend. She may well feel at ease with him, too, in a rather different way, for he heard what she said when her little boy was killed, and she thought for a moment that it was her lover. They were both called John.

Things were very different, naturally enough, in real life. Anthony Powell in his memoirs gives an excellent sketch of John Heygate, the man with whom Waugh's wife actually went off. In terms of Waugh's world nobody could have been more different from John Beaver. Heygate was good-looking, talented and popular, from an old family and with all the right schools and clubs. He seems to have had, too, just the right sort of dashing high spirits and fecklessness of which his social set would approve; for when news of the affair came out he was not with the wife he had removed from her husband, but travelling with Powell on the continent in his touring car.

A peremptory telegram from Waugh, who could be highly formidable in his own style, summoned him home to face the music. Heygate and Waugh's wife got married subsequently and the marriage was quite a success although it did not last. To earn money Heygate wrote a school novel which sold well, and he was also successful in the film world; but in later life he suffered breakdowns and fits of mental disturbance. That might have interested Waugh as the author of *The Ordeal of Gilbert Pinfold*; but in general Heygate was not a promising character for a novel, especially not a novel by Waugh. One can see why Waugh was inspired to create John Beaver, one of his best characters, and one to whom he could transfer the contemptible qualities which he would no doubt have liked to find in Heygate, but could not.

Tony Last's Victorian Gothic hall is obviously based on Madresfield House near Malvern, which Waugh knew well and felt as much affection for as Tony Last did for his own Gothic pile. Tony's presumed end in the Amazon jungles, captive of the dreadful Mr Todd, was suggested by Waugh's own experiences in Guyana, where he had gone exploring in an effort to forget about his failed marriage. The best of Waugh's excellent travel books is *Ninety-Two Days*, which he wrote about his South American experiences. Even the fictional Mr Todd is not as vivid as his counterpart in real life, the old hermit whom Waugh encountered in the jungle, who distracted his guest with theological speculation, and roamed around Waugh's hammock as he lay in the rain getting steadily drunk on rum. (This strange old man also rejected a medallion of the Virgin which Waugh offered him, saying 'Why should I require a picture of someone I see so frequently? Besides,' he added contemptuously, 'it is not in the least like her.')

When his wife leaves him and insists on a divorce Tony Last finds himself living 'in a world suddenly bereft of order', in which 'no outrageous circumstance he found himself in could add a jot to the all-encompassing chaos.' What ordinary widowers discover is a world not so intense and dramatic as that, and yet it is essentially similar. Even such books as I now read seem to reflect this. I can't manage Barbara Pym any more, whom I used to read with such pleasure. But I now feel as completely at home in Waugh's world as I used to do with Pym's spinsters and curates, and eccentrics of quite a different kind.

During a sleepless night after my return from Lanzarote I try to contrive a different kind of ending to Waugh's novel. Suppose Tony Last had woken up prematurely, after being drugged by Mr Todd to conceal him from the rescue party? It is essential to keep Mr Todd in the story: he is one of Waugh's most memorable creations. But if Tony Last had escaped from him what might have happened? The next scene would be back in England at Hetton, with Brenda now making much of the returned hero. As happy days go by she might have blandished Tony into settling some sort of capital sum or jointure on her. Tony is now eating out of her hand, but Brenda is still secretly in touch with John Beaver, and still loves him. Beaver is at a loose end, again ignored by the smart world who took him up as an object of interest after Brenda made him her young man.

When Brenda secures her jointure she invites him to marry her after she gets her divorce. Beaver is tempted. Her money is not much, but together and married they will get a place in the London smart set; they will be talked about. He agrees to do it after he gets back from an American trip with his mother. And over there he meets an heiress, very rich, very suitable, very easily taken in. Bully for Beaver. His bride-to-be rejoices at the prospect of life in Mayfair with an upper-class young Englishman. Mrs Beaver is delighted. She will keep her son; she will have the heiress in hand as part of her own show.

And what of Brenda? Deep down poor Brenda is a stoic; she knows when she is beaten. She cannot stop wanting her Beaver; perhaps she can still have him on the side? She thinks of him when she lets Tony make love to her and then she is pregnant again. On that note the alternative novel ends?

And about time too – daylight is showing outside. Waugh himself could never have written such a novel of course. His genius as an artist went quite another way and revelled in the grotesque horror of the conclusion he created. Tony Last, last of his kind, rescued from death by this jungle hermit with an insatiable lust to listen to the novels of Dickens, which he cannot read. And so while life back in England goes on, Tony is kept a prisoner by his terrible host and made to read novel after Dickens novel. For ever and ever.

Masterly. Waugh's inimitably cool manner makes it all plausible, as well as frightening. But with Waugh, character is at the disposition of dramatic effect. Had Henry James written *A Handful of Dust* he would have been more interested in the people themselves. He would have pondered the inwardness of Brenda and Beaver, of Tony too, as the last representative of a type and a tradition. He would have stifled any sensational denouement in the interest of human relations, 'which stop nowhere'.

Jamesian scrupulosity is of course not suited to the bitterness that Waugh felt at the time, in the pursuit of which he contrived a black outcome. But however superb an artist he could be, Waugh was a cynic as well. He was quite prepared to accommodate his American publisher and compose a different ending for an American readership who, as Scott Fitzgerald said, must always have a tragedy with a happy ending.

Waugh made his alternative solution absurdly snug. Tony Last, rather like Waugh himself in *Ninety-Two Days*, looks forward to catching the boat home, and to his first dinner at Wheeler's or the Savoy; perhaps, too, a reconciliation with Brenda. In London, in response to his telegram, he does indeed meet a repentant Brenda, more than anxious to escape the poor and solitary life-style to which she has been reduced. They travel back to Hetton together and are last seen eating muffins in the dining-car. Not like Brenda? Of course not; and Waugh has already made it abundantly clear how far the iron of her faithlessness had eaten into Tony's soul.

But the author has obviously decided that the snugger the scene the greater the underlying irony. And did he consider that the irony would be safely lost on his American readers? The fact that he misjudged them was shown by the great success in America of his much later satire, *The Loved One*, a black comedy about Californian funeral customs. And of course by that time the success of *A Handful of Dust* on both sides of the Atlantic had led to the restoration of the original ending.

CHAPTER EIGHT

Belial and his Friends

I cling with possessive loyalty to the Iris who had Alzheimer's disease, and whom I looked after during those years. The disease itself seems to belong to me, and I don't like other people having it, although when I go to those Alzheimer gatherings I enjoy the comradeship and the togetherness, and I feel like a veteran at an Old Soldiers' Reunion. I have given up trying to remember Iris as she was before she was ill. (She would sometimes say 'Here's Ginger' even when she could barely say anything else.) Walking round the block with Iris, and afterwards with Mella, I always looked at one house in particular, where my old teacher David Cecil used to live.

Other people's houses may be untidy, but they have an air of knowing what's what, of being house-wise, knowing what they can get away with. David's house was like that. It was a rented house, pseudo-Georgian, quite large enough for a family of five, six or seven including nanny and cook. Rachel Cecil liked going out on her bicycle to buy food but hated cooking it; she had a particular horror of onions. One result was that eating at Linton Road was hardly an exciting experience, although talking and drinking there was such fun. The standard tipple favoured by David was mixed dry and sweet vermouth, with as much gin as one could surreptitiously pour in for oneself during one of his rhapsodical flights. Not that he was a monologuist; he had a habit of suddenly shouting out 'What do you think?' and listening with an almost embarrassing intentness to what one thought, which was seldom of much interest. But as well as being the most comfortable person imaginable to talk with, he raised and inspired the spirits like champagne, or at least as champagne is supposed to do, though I have never found that it does.

Just as he required you to put in more gin yourself if you wanted it, conferring his approval, if he happened to notice, with an absent wave of the hand, so he was the reason why wit was in you: if it happened to be so it came from him, although it was yourself you thought was being so clever. He was like Falstaff, not only funny and delightful in himself but the reason why fun and delight were in others. Like the Duke in *Measure for Measure* too, who said he enjoyed seeing other people laugh and rejoice more than doing so himself. Possibly Shakespeare too was a bit like that, although it may be significant that it is the Duke in disguise who makes the claim. The Duke may really have been a rather priggish fellow, concerned only with his image in his own eyes, and in those of his subjects.

Iris was certainly and honestly more concerned to see other people happy then than to be happy herself. But the two went together, as they should. Iris loved to ask people what they did, and what they thought, and they were never slow to tell her.

I remember that; of course I do; but I can't remember *her*, as she did it. I can remember David Cecil perfectly: how he looked, how he turned his head like a bird, his every inflection and gesture. But the Iris of those days has gone from me.

Do others remember her better than I do? Much better? Probably. For me will she now always remain my Iris of the Alzheimer's? I don't know. There seems such a long way to go. And I've no idea whether the former Iris will ever come back, or how, or even if I want her to. Existlessness can't change much, even for the bereaved. The bereaved only become more and more obsessed with themselves, and with how they are taking it. And with their own image of the dead.

Perhaps that's the main reason why I can't now remember Iris, as she once was.

*

Memories are obsessions too, I suppose; but I like to think of David Cecil, and the things he said, and the stories he told. He was fond of Christopher Woodforde, the sardonic Chaplain of New College, who was sometimes displeased with him about something or other, and then addressed him, disapprovingly, as 'Lord David'. Christopher's great-however-many-times-grandfather was the Parson Woodforde who wrote the *Diaries*, which are chiefly concerned with what the Parson had every day for dinner.

The Parson's latter-day relative was not altogether a popular figure in the college, having an extremely sharp tongue; but he and David Cecil got on very well. Christopher's wife, who had the same tongue although she was both nice and kind, once amused David very much by her remark about Dr Cooke, the Fellow in Chemistry. David said to her how much he liked Dr Cooke, who was indeed a most amiable and estimable man.

'So do I,' replied Mrs Woodforde. 'But do you know, whenever I see him I imagine him wearing a white coat and wrapping me a bottle of cough mixture.'

Christopher Woodforde hated the College Warden, in a manner altogether disproportionate to that unfortunate man's capacity to be a nuisance, although indeed he could be one. When the Warden died Christopher gave an eloquent and touching address at the funeral – like many sardonic clergymen he was an excellent preacher – and afterwards he was congratulated on it by Alan Bullock (now Lord Bullock), the History Fellow. Giving him a venomous glance the Chaplain hissed: 'I hope the bastard is frying in hell.'

Bullock, a robust atheist of enlightened views, was deeply shocked by this unlooked-for depth of clerical ill-feeling, although it did not lessen his respect for the Chaplain as a man of what Hardy calls 'sound parish views'.

It was soon after this episode that David Cecil fell from grace in the eyes of Christopher Woodforde, never afterwards retrieving himself but becoming 'Lord David' from then on, although his habitual insouciance made him sublimely unconscious of the fact. It arose when he and his wife Rachel asked the Chaplain to dinner. Christopher knew very well that this would be a sparse and unattractive meal compared to the dinner he would get in college; but he was fond of the Cecils and prepared to renounce for once the solid comforts of his usual college evening. He was touched too, because his wife had recently died, and it was clear that the Cecils were anxious to help, and solicitous that he should not mope alone in his college rooms.

Christopher arrived punctually in Linton Road at the hour of invitation. As he opened the garden gate the front door was flung open and David and Rachel came out, obviously in a hurry. They swept past Christopher with a word of hasty apology, Rachel pausing for a moment to thank him for calling, and saying that he must come again soon.

'I didn't mind their forgetting so much,' the Chaplain explained to me later. 'What I really resented was that I had missed dinner in Hall. I didn't get my usual dinner, and I didn't even get whatever concoction would have been served up by the Cecils.'

He bore no malice for the incident, beyond reverting to that formal style of address when addressing David Cecil. But there was certainly no doubt that Christopher could be a champion hater if he wanted. Later, when he had retired from New College and become Dean of Wells, he sometimes asked Iris and me to stay with him and his son Giles at the Deanery. Giles was an odd but likeable boy whose hobby – it was more like a vocation – was to visit and make a record of every cinema which had a teashop attached. Once almost universal, the cinema tea-lounge was then a vanishing amenity, and Giles's passion was to draw up an exhaustive list of them for the sake of posterity, and before they had all disappeared, carefully noting what kind of buns were served, and whether the waitresses wore a uniform.

His father meanwhile waged a ferocious war against the doddery old Canons in the Close, singling out one who was especially harmless and amiable for bouts of intensive persecution.

'I hate that man,' he confided to Iris and me when his enemy was seen toddling along before us in the Close. 'I'm going to have him *shot out*.'

Christopher never specified how this dire deed – pronounced with an explosive hiss – was to be accomplished; and I imagine that the old Canon remained happily oblivious of the fate that was allegedly hanging over him. Christopher was not exactly kind-hearted at bottom, but one could be sure that threats and imprecations, alarming as they might sound in the mouth of a distinguished churchman (he had written the definitive work on ecclesiastical stained glass), would never in practice produce any serious consequences.

I thought of Christopher Woodforde, and the aborted dinner party, when I had myself begun to suffer the well-meaning persecution to which widowers appeared to be subject. Many times in these weeks, as I presented myself at some hospitable front door, I remembered what had happened to Christopher, and thought how lucky in one sense at least he had been. He might have missed his dinner, but he had escaped the evening; and what a relief it would often be for me if my putative hosts had left as I arrived, with the hasty wish that they might see me again soon. I should have wandered thankfully home, and enjoyed my usual supper of sardines or scrambled eggs …

*

And now the burglars have been.

Their visit was like a tonic. It seemed, too, absolutely the right thing to happen in a widower's house. Part of a ritual, like the interment, or the wake, or the memorial service. And wasn't there a time when they read the will?

I can almost imagine responsible burglars saying to one another in a concerned sort of way: 'It's high time we paid that call on Mr Bayley. It's quite a while now since his good lady died. Don't want to leave it too long. You free tonight, George? Good. In that case …'

We never had the burglars before, even when there were the two of us here. Several houses round about were burgled – we knew all about it – and on one occasion I found traces of a not very convincing attempt to break in. Our neighbours had burglar alarms, but I shrank from the technology involved, the tedium of setting it and at least partly understanding it, the annoyance to everybody when it went off by mistake. Someone suggested, not altogether seriously, that we get a dummy burglar alarm. This seemed to me a good idea. I have always been attracted by pretence. A successful fraud; something, in this case, just as good as the real thing. Besides, in those days it would have given us something to do; probably for the whole of one morning.

That was two years ago. Iris had not yet reached the stage of incoherence and unpredictability. It had not yet occurred to me to keep the doors locked on the inside; up to that point there had been no need to do so. She still enjoyed going out in the car and for both of us it was better than staying at home.

We went to a huge Do-It-Yourself store in the outskirts of the town. The place, I had been advised, to buy these funny things, which were made in Korea, or perhaps in Singapore. When, after endless wanderings among forests of lampshades and electrical fixtures we chanced on an assistant preoccupied with some papers but prepared to lend us an ear, I found him at first baffled, but then disapproving. He was clearly disposed to find the whole notion improper and irregular. Such a low-down idea discredited the mystery of the do-it-yourself trade.

I saw his point, and began to feel it was bad form to make such a request. But at last the assistant relented and indicated a row of cardboard cartons on a shelf. He asked me to refrain from opening the thing in the shop. I wondered if this was to avoid compromising the security of my house; but it seemed more likely that the man wanted no further part in what he considered an under-the-counter transaction, alien to the clean-living ethos of the store. Feeling shamefaced I paid, and we took the box home.

When I got the dummy alarm out I saw at once what the objection was. No one, let alone a burglar, could possibly be taken in by this. Even the gadgets and the lettering which attempted to give it a semblance of reality were flashy and overdone. 'Spyder Alarms' it said; and the spider portrayed was a spirited, even a threatening creature. And yet no burglar could possibly have felt threatened by it.

The burglars probably never even bothered to look at it. They came when I was away for a day or two with my brother Michael and a friend. Some days earlier a nice old man had been trimming off the ivy from a neighbouring wall. He rang the bell and suggested that a huge bush which was straggling up the side of the house might also be profitably trimmed a little. I had to agree with him, and he did a good and unobtrusive job, not bothering me at all. The height of the bush required him to use a ladder. He removed the debris in an ancient van. A nice job, tidy and not expensive.

When I got back from my two-day absence I didn't notice anything different at first. Widowers' houses probably get to have a look inside as if nothing has ever changed, or could change. Then I went to turn a standard lamp on and found it wasn't there.

Well, natural enough. 'Pieland' had got it. Probably wouldn't be back, but I could do without it. In fact it got in the way rather. I only used it when I had to telephone. A bit odd though. In fact, come to think of it, distinctly odd.

Only when I went upstairs to the bedroom – our bedroom – did I get a real shock. The big oak chest which stood by the window and prevented one looking out and was layers and layers deep with books and old *London Review*s and socks and things – the chest wasn't there either. Where had we got it? Many years ago, in some half antique, half junk shop. Cheap. Probably the reason why we got it; Iris could never resist something like that.

What was inside it? No idea, haven't looked in it for years. Always far too much lying on the top. But there must have been something inside it, indeed quite a lot, because my eye now takes in a new mass of stuff – the usual sorts of stuff, quite tidily disposed all round about; everywhere, in fact, except on the more than usually dirty patch where the great chest once stood. With a feeling of liberation – nice to be able to move about freely – I went to the window to open it. No, it was already open. That's funny. The security lock was dangling rather elegantly by one screw. No other damage.

At this moment I remembered Mr Sullivan, the nice old gentleman who had been clearing the bush off the wall. Surely not. And how on earth? Well, it certainly looked like it. Moving more alertly now around the house I began to realise how much had gone. Two large oak chests, one of which had contained our collection of old 78 and 33 records, which had now been neatly stacked on the ragged drawing-room carpet. The French tapestry armchair which Iris had bought for me ten years ago, on my sixty-fourth birthday. Even that old friend, the Windsor chair in the kitchen on which I had twice caught my tail when coming down to make tea in the morning. I began to notice numerous other gaps – small tables, vases, ornaments, a few pictures.

The TV and the video, which I had never managed to work, were still sitting in their corner. Untouched and unwanted.

But what a relief that Iris was not here to see that her treasures had gone! She would have been *so* upset. More than upset. Indignant, sad, miserable, even furious for a while. The fury she would have concealed, knowing that it would upset me; but she would have felt it inside all the more. I mean of course if the burglary had happened before she was ill. Towards the end she would not have seen nor noticed anything. And I should not have told her.

I began to realise now how dismayed I felt that I didn't feel anything. Not only dismayed but frightened as well. I didn't care. The things were gone; I wasn't interested in them. Was I interested in *anything* any more? The disappearance of the things made the question abruptly and alarmingly meaningful.

I pushed it aside and began to think about the things themselves. Wasn't it a relief that so much had gone, particularly those two great chests? But think of the labour of getting them out of the house! And why on earth should they have wanted them? I was told afterwards that antique oak furniture, even semi-antique oak furniture, is extremely valuable today. Well, so much the better for that nice Mr Sullivan.

Could one be sure that it had been Mr Sullivan? He might well have tipped off his friends, supplied the van and the local knowledge. And I remembered now that I had given him the key to the padlock of the side gate, so that he could come and go. He had apologised that he had lost the padlock – must have dropped it somewhere – and he had brought another padlock and given me the key. One key, I now realised; the other one he must have kept.

When the police came a day or two later, and asked me whether I had any ideas, I enquired rather diffidently if it was all right to mention a possible suspect. By all means, they said. And when I explained about the bush being trimmed off the wall, and who had performed this service, they chuckled, and one of them remarked wearily: 'Oh, we know Mr Sullivan.'

I felt inclined to ask why, in that case, they didn't do something about him; but then I remembered that in England suspicion, no matter how overwhelming, is not enough. Besides, the policemen gave me the decided impression that they would much rather not do anything about Mr Sullivan. It would involve too much work, as well as being rather unsporting. Instead they suggested that I should have the services of a counsellor, which they would be more than happy to arrange. A counsellor for what, I asked? The shock, they explained.

After they had gone I started to wonder about that. Was I feeling any shock? The answer seemed to be no – absolutely none at all. What had happened seemed an entirely natural – even inevitable – part of my new existence. One could hardly call it my new life-style. Anything that happened from now on, good, bad and indifferent, cancer, a car smash, a gigantic legacy, a best-selling novel, months and years of quiet total boredom – somehow it would all be the same.

And for some reason it was not a depressing prospect. Like the disappearance of the furniture, I faced it with a mild sense of relief. There were other things that had happened in the course of bereavement about which I was far from feeling the same sort of equanimity. For instance, the gradual vanishing of that old desire for my evening drink. And the looking forward to it. Now I pour something out with languor and lack of appetite. Might as well have a drink as anything else. That's not the way to go about it.

The drink had been part of my old routine. The routine of looking after Iris, which had blessed existence with reality. Now it was just existence. One thing or one person was now as real or as unreal as the next.

If only I could be thoroughly independent, free from all these daily fidgets and anxieties and exasperations which have suddenly got so bad ... Why didn't I have them before, when Iris was ill? Why couldn't I settle down to the *propriety* of bereavement, which should surely have its own spare and dignified emptiness of routine? Like being a monk, even a Trappist monk.

Being bereaved is not a career, like teaching or acting. I can see that. But I wish it were. How much more comfortable if it were a recognised profession, one of those

> in which men engage –
> The army, the navy, the church or the stage ...

Isn't life happily like that in one of those Gilbert and Sullivan operas? I would like to be *engaged* in bereavement. An exacting job but a rewarding one, after the arduous period of preliminary training.

Or even if it isn't a career there must be some ideal way of doing it. A way of living I could aspire to, a Platonic vision of the widowed state?

Iris, who was such a deep and wise student of Plato, would be amused by that. But, I suppose, as things are, this is just the untidy, scuffling, scuttling way of living that bereavement must be for everybody.

How would I set about finding out? I don't want to find out.

*

Now I am missing the attacks of grief, which once came on with the suddenness of asthma or toothache. With the difference that each had an indescribable and physical happiness about it. More like sex in a way than misery; and yet so sharp and so agonising that each felt as if it would have been impossible to bear without the rush of tears and hiccups that accompanied it. I am sure that some people suffer the agony without those relieving symptoms: but I don't see how they do it.

As with most other things in life it is impossible to imagine or to be sure how other people are taking it. All experience is private, however universal, yet this one must in its own way be a special case. Between attacks, as it were, I remember thinking that all widows and widowers must undergo the same sort of symptoms, just as patients who have the same disease must do.

The condition of bereavement is well-defined. Less well-defined, possibly, is the wonderful sense of being alive that grief confers on its patient. Now, a year after Iris died, I miss that aliveness more than anything.

I miss other symptoms of aliveness too. The frenzies of rage and despair which came on sometimes before Iris died, in the same way that the fits of grief came on afterwards. And the fits of love too, during the months before her death, as wonderful and as physical as any experience in life could be.

Life – that's it. I haven't lived since the grief began to go away, and that is why I miss it so much.

And yet talking about 'life' in this way always sounds bogus. D.H. Lawrence was apt to do it, and his disciples and admirers were always talking about being 'on the side of life', whatever that means. Lawrence *was* alive, oh yes, and one can feel it as if not only in his words and his style but in his actual sensations, as if the two were the same. But talking about 'life' in that reverent way is another matter. It takes away the thing itself.

I feel not only that I have not been living since grief, now so much missed, started to go away, but that I haven't wanted to live. I preferred the other thing: just waiting to die. But the tranquillity of death, which I hoped to get into my daily experience, has proved to be something of an illusion. A nice, quiet, settled existence of routines, and little things presenting themselves throughout the day; that was what I was always harping on to myself. And nothing came of it. Naturally enough perhaps. Nothing except trouble, as it now seems, in various forms. Trouble like Margot and Mella. And did I, without knowing it, need that trouble? As a man in the desert needs water?

The chief comfort of my imagined way of being a widower had been quietly to look forward to each thing, each minute *being over*, while it was still actually going on. Anticipation as an end in itself, a goal and centre for consciousness? But what about that fallen but persuasive archangel, Belial? He wanted a quiet time too, but a quiet time for simple intellectual indulgence, for those 'thoughts that wander through eternity'. These, like those outbursts of grief, seem to me now no longer a part of daily existence. Why this should be so is not easy to say. Perhaps because they were an involuntary indulgence, like grief itself? My vision of the ideal widower's regime is that nothing should be involuntary. It should all have been arranged beforehand, by myself, for myself.

The chief danger to such a regime is its vulnerability. I had known Margot and Mella for years! Well – for a long time anyway. How could I have known that they would start to behave in the way they did? My own behaviour, in response to theirs, was, I like to think, far more predictable. Predictable, yes – but also extremely shabby? And yet could I really have behaved in any other way? I don't see that I could. My desire, at all costs, was to keep my widower's house intact. Granted that wish, all the rest follows.

During the last year I have become in my own eyes a more unattractive character, and, what is worse, a more boring one. Boring to myself, un-nice in my own interior being. ('Un-nice' is a coinage of Audi's, from the days of we four [or we three] being together. It is also possible to be 'un-nasty' in the same spirit.)

Iris and I used to be 'bad' with great pleasure and frequency. She or I would say: 'Bad animal!' to the other, and this was a reassurance and a compliment, although Iris would often say as if in protest 'I am *not* a bad animal!' and I would reply: 'Course you're not a bad animal!' Good and bad naturally meant more to Iris, as a philosopher, than they did to me.

'It's a bit wonkmouse,' I used to say to Iris, who took the point of the word for my sake. Words with the suffix 'mouse' were OK words, which pleased us more for themselves than for what they signified. 'Wonkmouse' indicated something one was trying to do, and not succeeding, and deciding in consequence that it probably wasn't worth doing anyway. I was very definitely a wonkmouse man, whereas for Iris wonkmousery was only acceptable for the pair of us together, and for our joint activities. The more 'mouse' these were the better, for 'mouse' meant everything we took for granted and did together, without even being conscious of the fact that we did.

Iris, however, without ever being 'un-mouse', was in her own world completely separated from mouse activities. Her work was as much shut off from ordinary mouse activities as it was in itself deliberate and mysterious. This sense of her wholly separate being was to me the greatest source of pleasure and relaxation that our marriage afforded. On the Sparrow and Dog principle, it was almost as good as not being married at all.

I once teased Iris by telling her that she must have taken her own sort of vows when we got married.

'You're right,' she said. 'It was such a nice moment. Getting married to you meant I could give up living, and all that love business, and start doing my work.'

An exaggeration of course, but it was true that Iris's sense of life, however different from that of Dostoevsky or D.H. Lawrence, was in its own way an equally positive affair, which included loving, suffering, pitying, tormenting and being tormented – all the standard ingredients of passion and ecstasy, guilt and misery and desire. What she had called 'love business' most of all. She had lived life, as the saying is, to the full: and now she was going to write about it.

Which she did, and had done. For me, living with Iris, as she was with me and for me, was quite enough. Year by happy year, as it had been for me, while we had grown ever 'closer and closer apart'. I had no conscious desire for life in any fuller or more absolute sense. But while she was very ill, and after she died, the aliveness began. The rage, the suffering and the grief. I was not exactly surprised by it, but without conscious reflection I decided I must get rid of it somehow. I must achieve that patterned existence of quiet, empty, solitary routines.

I never had. And while all the business with Mella and Margot was going on I had those frequent moments of panic and emptiness that made it clear to me that I didn't, after all, really want to be left on my own.

What was I to do then? To be a widower in my own house, with my

171

own routines and thoughts, had been my ideal. I had behaved ingloriously where Mella and Margot were concerned, in order to retain that way of being, and to keep it safe. And now it seemed that I didn't want it after all.

But I *must* do! For what else was there? Even those thoughts, the thoughts that wander through eternity, taking in on their way such interesting objects of speculation as the Krag-Jörgensen rifle, and the historic battle of Svold, which I had once or twice discussed with Audi – even these thoughts had lately begun to pall. It was a pity, because I was genuinely interested in the battle of Svold. It was fought in the year 1000, a thousand years before our own tedious millennium.

That rash and glorious Viking Olaf Tryggvason, who in his youth had beaten the English army at Maldon on the Essex marshes, had then won his way to his kingdom in Norway. Now he was throwing it away in a mad expedition to extract a great dowry from the Danish king, Svein Forkbeard, for his wife, the king's daughter, whom Olaf had married against the king's will. He knew that Svein Forkbeard had allied himself with the king of Sweden, and with malcontents from his own Norway, but he did not care. He did not care even when it was clear that they had ambushed him off the island of Svold, or when he saw the size of their fleet ...

What matter? In his great ship, the *Long Serpent*, the biggest longship in the north, he would fight them off. And if he failed? Well, he failed, and went down to Valhalla fighting gloriously as a Viking should. (He remembered now and then that he was supposed to have been converted to Christianity; he had given up raiding England because it was a Christian country; but in this last fight he would have put all that out of his mind.)

His comrade Einar Tamberskelver was beside him on the poop of the *Long Serpent*, which towered above the remainder of his little flotilla. Einar was a crack archer, and had been picking off the opposition with his deadly arrows. But a Finn in the Swedish fleet, a skilled warlock like all Finns, contrived to pierce Einar's bowstring with a magic arrow. Between blows at Swedish and Danish heads Olaf asked what had caused the resounding twang he had just heard.

Einar then, the arrow taking
From the loosened string,
Answered 'That was Norway breaking
'Neath thy hand, O king.'

Longfellow, the American poet, does that part of the old chronicle in
his poem very well. As the greatest warship in the north was system-
atically boarded and overwhelmed by the enemy, Olaf struck down a
last opponent, jumped from the stern with his sword in his hand and
in all his armour, and was never seen again. He was long looked for
and prayed for. After the battle Norway was overrun by Swedes and
Danes, but although his countrymen prayed to Christ and Odin for
his return 'Olaf Tryggvason never came back to his kingdom.'

Suddenly that seems to me overwhelmingly sad. Why? I don't care
a curse about others – kings, princes, pretenders – who never came
back to their countries. When he drowned at Svold was Olaf's father
still alive? The cunning old fox, Trygve of the Vik, the Vik being the
fjord that led to the town of Oslo. That may be the reason why Vikings
are called Vikings, though the point is disputed.

'Is it now?' as Iris would say. She would have looked and listened
to me with smiling indulgence. And now what should I care? But if I
give up caring about thoughts like that, where should I be? I wish Olaf
had won his last battle. He was only trying, for himself of course, to
get a queen's dowry for his new wife. Her father must have been that
Svein Forkbeard who became king of York, and whose son, the great
Knut (Canute to us) made himself king of England. King of Denmark
too of course. Who was it told me that a verse in the Danish National
Anthem still celebrates that fact? 'Once we ruled England ...'?

How I wish I could tell Iris all this! Talk about it to her, as I would
have done once, many years ago. She never minded my rambling on
to her about something of absolutely no importance at all. She used
to say she liked it. She used to sit looking at me with a smile on her
face, and I could see she was herself thinking of something important.
Something worthwhile. That used to give me such pleasure.

Curious that when Iris was ill these Belial thoughts that wander about were my great solace, indeed my greatest pleasure. Did I think that I was still sharing them with Iris? I don't think so. It's only now, when she's not here, that I want her to be here, so that I could share them with her.

Olaf's new wife, the Danish princess, was his third. I fancy his first was a Wend. No doubt a Wendish princess. They thought a lot about royal blood in those days; took its importance for granted, if they happened to have it themselves. The Viking aristocracy bled to death in civil wars ...

This is becoming a nightmare. Never mind the Viking aristocracy, I feel as if I were bleeding to death myself. What is wrong with me nowadays? I wouldn't want to ask Mella or Margot, those ghost figures from a more recent past. From a past that is more distant to me than Iris. I seem to be losing all sense of the past; and with it all the thoughts that cocooned me round when I was looking after Iris, and which I thought I could still depend upon, now that she is gone. It seems I can't. And I can't now even remember how long she has been gone for.

*

Head spinning round and round, I must stop it. There must be something left, something to hold on to? That last Christmas, for instance? No, it had better not be that last Christmas. What about the one before? And now, of course, I am vividly remembering both of them, but particularly the one which I didn't want to remember.

Michael comes to fetch us in his car. On Christmas morning, when he goes off as usual to Chelsea Old Church, I hope that Iris and I could do our usual walk to Kensington Gardens. But Iris is so much weaker. We get as far as Kensington Gardens, and it was not far, but once there we have to sit down. No question of the Serpentine. We sit down, and lean ourselves together, and twine our hands. I say to Iris: '*Poujin?*'

I am smiling at her, hoping she will reply. It is a word she invented herself, or seemed to invent, about three months earlier. It was in the

174

car; she turned and put her hand on my knee, and said, with some emphasis, sounds or words, two of which sounded like 'Poujin'. She seemed to think the word an important one, and she looked happy while she said it.

But now, however many times I hopefully repeat 'Poujin', Iris's eye and face gives no flicker of recognition. The word-sound has gone, and will not return. She looks vacantly into the distance. But then in a moment or two she seems to be looking at something.

She is. It is the Albert Memorial, newly washed and cleaned and painted and gilded, so that it shines like an eastern temple in the weak winter sunshine. It was foggy when we got to the park and found our seat, which faced down Queen's Gate. We did not notice the Memorial; in any case, I have quite given up thinking that Iris might notice things. I take it for granted that she cannot.

But she has. She has seen the sun-gilt back of the Prince Consort, vast and cloaked in his scrubbed new imperial majesty. He is looking away from London, sitting on his chair or throne or whatever it is, and gazing placidly over the green stretches of the park, as if they were his own German fields.

I wonder what it was like, that Christmas at Windsor. There was probably a big and boring dinner party going on, when Albert felt the first feverish symptoms of typhoid. If typhoid gives you feverish symptoms. All I had to go on was Virginia Woolf's first and best novel, *The Voyage Out*, in which the heroine, Rachel, dies of typhoid. She has just become engaged to be married and is very happy but rather giddy and distracted. She has a headache. For coolness she puts her hand on the metal globe which ornaments her bed, and soon finds that it has become uncomfortably hot ...

Virginia Woolf knew all about it, because her brother Thoby had died of typhoid. In their house somewhere just across the park there.

Iris has no further interest in the Prince Consort. Probably it was only his gilded back that caught her attention. I hug her and say 'Poujin!' once more, but for her it is only some incomprehensible word-sound. Her face puckers, and the anxious look, so far absent this

Christmas morning, comes back over it, like clouds beginning to come back over the sun.

As indeed they are. I shiver, but Iris doesn't seem aware of the cold.

I smile at her, reassuringly, I hope. She was always young, and still looks youthful enough to live for ever. This dreadful childhood has come upon her as if she were Peter Pan himself. Peter Pan is eternally youthful; and here broods the still comely Prince Consort, looking as if he had never been young. Marriage to a queen robbed him of that chance, poor man. The irony of it seems worse this year than last year, when I could talk away to Iris beside the Serpentine statue, not indeed in the hope that she could join in, but with the feeling, given confidence by her own eyes and smile – however timid and uncertain these had become – that my chatter still reassured her, as it had always done in the past.

Not now: not any longer. As we walk along together I talk absently to myself, without even turning my head to see if the words have any effect on Iris. But then I pull myself together and ask if she enjoyed seeing Albert? All done up in his new gilt cloak?

'Albert, darling?' I say hopefully.

Iris waves her head, still smiling. Two big tears peer out under her eyelids and then slide down her cheeks. The sight is extraordinarily reassuring, as satisfying as if it were some much more intimate bodily process of my own. I seize her round the waist and dance a few steps with her, kissing both her cheeks. We go along together arm in arm.

But why Albert? 'Peter Pan?' I say hopefully. And then 'Poujin?' To neither of these does Iris make any response. Albert is the one she fancies. A dashing name? At one time it could have had the glow and the sweet nostalgia of a first remembered love ...

But not for Iris surely? Only if she had lived in those old Victorian days, for which she would now have to be about a hundred and something instead of a mere seventy-nine.

Being a 'carer' is in one sense a wholly incurious business. Curiosity about the behaviour of the person you look after seems to dry up and die, as if it was as much as you could do to look after them as they appear to be, and attend to their needs mechanically and without attention. I was fascinated for a moment, none the less, by Iris's Albert response. It was like operating the machine cluelessly and at random, and suddenly making it disgorge a mass of coins or tokens. At one time I had hoped 'Poujin' – Iris's own word – would prove similarly rewarding, but no.

I clung to Poujin all the same. Iris had given it to me, even if she didn't want it herself. I felt, quite arbitrarily of course, that she had intended to convey something about our present relations to each other. I was her Poujin, as it might be a husband or a 'carer', even, as it might have been in the days of Albert, her 'young man', or with a change of sex a 'best girl'. It was, at least, a more vigorous and somehow a more expressive word than the deadly dull and null 'carer', with its whiff of Welfare State correctness. I mentioned Poujin once at an Alzheimer meeting, and Dr Jacoby suggested we should all become Poujins, instead of carers.

*

It was our last Christmas. And Albert must have had his last Christmas too. At Windsor, where the drains were so bad. The Queen wouldn't have cared or noticed. She could have stood any amount of infection from drains.

Our last Christmas. And Iris, although I had no idea of it, had less than two months to live. Did she wish to live? Or was she content, all unconsciously as Albert may have been, to let life slip away?

About the middle of January she stopped eating or drinking. Nothing I could do would persuade her to take in as much as even a teaspoonful of milk. And she was very merry about it. She smiled at me in an almost roguish way as I coaxed and cajoled. It could hardly have been a death-wish, because Iris had long since passed the point where any wish or desire could come into her head, or into her voice. She was not wanting to die. But she seemed to have received secret orders, which at once filled her with a secret joy. She could do what they suggested; she could fulfil their requirements to the letter.

So I took her to Vale House, that wonderful Home. It was always full up, and I was extremely lucky to get her in; only someone dying there made it possible. There seemed nothing else to do, but I was in terror none the less in case she should be so miserable, perhaps even violent (which she never had been), that I should have to find something else, some other way of dealing with the situation.

But Iris was happy. Her face lit up like an angel's when I appeared every morning, but this seemed not because of me but because she was so happy that she showed her happiness to me like a child. She even permitted herself to relax a little those invisible orders she had received. Not officially as it were. She still refused anything we tried to give her. But if I and the Irish nurse sat beside her she would wait until we were deep in talk and paying her no attention, and then suddenly swoop on the spoon we were holding and suck a little milk from it. Then she would look inimitably sly. She wanted us not to have noticed, but at the same time to admire what she had done, and the clever way she had done it.

But after a while, a short while, she seemed to think she had amused us long enough. She was as merry and courteous as ever, but there could be no further compromise, even for our pleasure. It was time to go.

And so she went. No death-wish – how could there have been? But terminal illness may at moments give the impression of one. Alzheimer's most of all. The brain and body seem so far apart, and the body seems to issue its own orders, as if saying, 'I am perfectly capable of carrying on. But why should I?'

*

Nobody *really* wants what they want. Or, to put it another way, everyone unconsciously rejects the image of themselves and their doings which they know to be most desirable and proper for them. I knew, all those years and years ago, that I was making a great mistake in marrying Iris. Every instinct about myself that I recognised and valued told me not to do it.

But it seems that I did do it. I jumped. I jumped where I should have stayed still, and I was sure, quite sure, that doing nothing was the thing for me to do.

So the forty-four years that mostly constituted my adult life had been determined by doing the very thing I was sure I didn't want to do? Good. And of course it is a familiar and indeed a banal story. Lots and lots of people have done, or are doing, just the same thing. And with the same wholly satisfactory results. A life lived and in no way regretted can only be satisfactory: both for those who lived it, and in the eyes of anyone who has happened to notice them.

Now, as a widower, I again found myself in the position of being able to do what I wanted. And this time I didn't have to make a choice. I could do what I knew I wanted to do without being confronted or threatened with an alternative. There was no alternative. Even Mella and Margot, distracting as their ministrations had been, had only deflected at a superficial level my wish to lead my own widower's life.

But widowers, as I was finding out, don't lead lives. They wait for something to happen: and when something does happen it becomes a muddle from which they at once have to try to escape.

That at least was my experience. I had tried to make a life – almost a 'Life' – out of being a widower, and it had led into this vertigo of anxiety, a state which I found myself comparing more and more with the state of anxiety to which Iris had first succumbed with the onset of Alzheimer's.

However blasphemous the comparison might be I couldn't help making it. Day and night now I was haunted by the sound of things we had said together in earlier times; by the smile she wore in her last days, by the way she lay in her bed on that last afternoon. Her last afternoon as herself. Since then she had been memories, images in the mind, words in books.

And those memories were pressing upon me with a greater and greater urgency. For the first time I longed to ask another widow or widower whether it was, or had been, the same for them. But as it happened I didn't know any recently bereaved persons: a surprising fact, it occurred to me, considering my age, and that of my contemporaries. Why was nobody dying at the moment? But it didn't matter, because I knew quite well that if I had known someone in my own position, the last thing I should have done would be to ask questions of this kind. Or of any kind. The bereaved should maintain the privacy and, in their own eyes, the singularity of their status. A privilege not to be transgressed.

*

I might be feeling more and more desperate but I was also getting more and more pompous. Was it because I had no one to think of but myself? No doubt. I actually needed now *more* harassment from other people, even from people like Mella and Margot. In my nice quiet widower's regime, which I had been so sure I wanted, depression was rising every day, as stealthily as floodwater.

I answered the phone now whenever it rang. I sat hoping for a call. And at last there was one! A nice foreign female voice which said something about Brussels. At once I felt harassed again, but almost happily harassed. I could not make out, however, what she was saying or what she wanted.

After we had rung off, with what must have been mutual relief, I felt I had had my adventure for the day, enough indeed for several days. I rather hoped to hear more, none the less, and I was not disappointed. Next morning there was a letter, with a Belgian stamp and a Brussels postmark. Thank goodness for the post!

The letter inside was headed 'Saint Amour'. Who was Saint Amour? Perhaps, with that ironical name, he was going to come and cure all my widower's problems.

In fact it turned out to be some kind of theatrical enterprise which was inviting me to take part in a series of performances 'on the theme of Love'. These would consist of authors, mainly Flemish, reading from their work. It was suggested that I should read some extracts from my memoir of Iris.

Of course I would give them a polite refusal. No other possibility entered my head. So certain was I of this decision that harassment and vertigo disappeared and left me feeling quite calm. This unnatural state of calm had unforeseen consequences. It must have had; because a week later I found myself walking into the Hotel Metropole in Brussels.

How had I got there? I seemed hardly to know myself. But I recalled that I had picked up the telephone and got through to Saint Amour in Brussels with dream-like ease. Before I knew what had happened, they had arranged the journey, and it was so simple.

The train slid under the Channel. Northern France looked as huge and desolate as Siberia, and I contemplated it with approval as I drank some wine and ate one of those long crusty '*sandwichs*' which I had always, but apparently mistakenly, supposed that the French called '*tartines*'. The landscape suited my mood, and so did the sandwich and the wine.

But how had it happened? I had thought that I would never again leave the widower's house; at least not voluntarily. And here I sat on a train in France. Feeling quite happy about it. Perhaps Iris had arranged the whole thing? I clung to that notion.

However my heart sank as I entered the Metropole. It was like coming back to school, and that was more than sixty years ago. It made me shed my widowerhood instantly. Here was all the awkwardness of the first day of term, after the unhappy arrival by train. True, the Hotel Metropole itself was not like school. It was vast and highly ornamented and full of *art nouveau* and monotonous great mirrors. But it must have been the experience of going back to school – coming back rather – which had suddenly exorcised widowerhood.

Images of school persisted. When I crept out to find somewhere to eat, for it was now past eight o'clock, I obtained a simple but satisfying meal at a café called The Rugbyman. My dish was a large quantity of tiny brown shrimps in their shells. As I crunched them with appetite they gave off a delicious aroma of saltmarsh and sandy northern beaches – the odours of my childhood. They were accompanied by Belgian 'white beer', a pallid but delicious brew, with a slice of lemon stuck tastefully on the rim of the big glass. It looked like ginger beer and was perfectly in keeping with the school tuckshop image; but it was very much stronger, as I soon found out.

On the following morning we answered our names to the Saint
Amour 'schoolmasters' in the lounge of the Metropole. The name of
the enterprise now seemed wonderfully well suited to the new school
I had been sent to, in my new adolescent and unwidowed persona. It
must be one of those fictional establishments about which boys and
girls used to read in school stories. 'The end of term play at Saint
Amour' – there was always fierce competition to be one of the cast,
perhaps even to shine as a star. I remembered from long ago reading
about the exploits of 'the worst girl at St Chad's', and all those
gripping doings which took place at St Dominic's.

The role of school matron was taken at our performances during
the week by a dark-featured, strikingly tall girl, whom I privately
christened the Angel of Death. Apart from nurse-maiding and feeding
us and driving the minibus to the towns where the show was to take
place, it was her duty, and by no means an unarduous one, to flush out
delinquent performers from some adjacent bar or café when their
number on the programme was imminent.

As the week went on, and the author-readers became more
accustomed to their roles in the production, the Angel of Death had
to work harder than ever, sometimes appearing as I was about to
raise a glass to my lips to march me back rapidly into the tartaric
sub-regions of the theatre. But once I had become accustomed to
her slightly sinister appearance and her imperious forefinger I
became quite fond of the Angel of Death; and her smile for me grew
more indulgent as the week went by, probably because my number
was the last on the list, and signalled the end of our labours for the
evening. My attachment seemed all the more suitable by reason of
the boarding school atmosphere in which we moved; no doubt I
had unknown rivals among the rest of the cast. We were all on very
jolly terms together, and like a busload of schoolboys we always
chorused a fond farewell to the Angel as she dropped us off at the
Metropole, well after midnight.

The show itself remained largely incomprehensible to me, partly
because none of us saw much of it outside our own particular acts.
Undertaken in the furtherance of Flemish culture it was entitled

Behoude de Begeerte, a sonorous and harmonious phrase which meant something like 'Hold on to the Passions'. For love, in its various obsessions and diversities, was the theme. A lively young Flemish author started us off by reading an extract from his book about the affection – perhaps more than affection – between a grandfather and granddaughter. The evening continued with another author's passion for his car, went on to examine crushes between girls, and those between younger and older men, culminating in a best-selling French writer's account of the joys of sex in a jacuzzi. I followed him as the last number on the bill, and was kindly described in a newspaper review as the 'Nestor of the company'.

As we read, our words appeared translated into Flemish on a giant screen behind our heads. Our invisible audience must have been bemused and not infrequently bored, but they remained kindly disposed, and gave us all a vigorous clap towards the end, when it dawned on them that the interminable evening – the show lasted more than three hours – was nearly over. It was strange to sit on a deckchair in the darkness, the Angel of Death hovering nearby in the eerie light of a blue bulb, waiting for my cue. The measured French tones from the stage would cease and I would prepare to read to an audience I never saw about the joys and woes of looking after Iris, the Alzheimer patient whom I had, indeed, so much loved.

Back in England, I could scarcely believe that this strange interlude had taken place. I hoped, vainly as it turned out, that my widower's house would now seem real, and interruptions to my platonic regime of widowerhood, the idea of which I still clung to in my mind, would vanish like the dance of those Chinese shadows. Mella, Margot, Saint Amour and *Behoude de Begeerte* – none of them *were* real, surely? The only real thing was an immense great hard sausage, or salami, that I had not been able to resist buying on my last day in Brussels. Its sheer size and weight made it an object of comfort. Caressing it sadly in the kitchen at home I remembered Audi poking knowledgeably about among the charcuterie in her local supermarket.

'I want something strong enough to kill a Swede,' she had observed with her angelic smile.

This, it seemed, was an ancient and neighbourly Norwegian proverb.

*

Apart from the sausage one other thing seemed weighty and worthwhile – even true. I had managed to visit a gallery before leaving Belgium, and I had seen the Virgin on her deathbed, in the picture by Van der Goes. It was like Iris on her deathbed. Perhaps it was like all of us on our deathbeds, but I thought only of Iris then. I failed to buy a postcard of that picture, but at the time it filled me with comfort.

There was a moment long ago on our honeymoon when we discovered, almost by accident, the little Italian town of Borgo St Sepolcro, and saw in its original setting in the town hall the fresco of the Resurrection by Piero della Francesca. Gazing vacantly at Van der Goes's Virgin I recalled that very different moment of her son's triumph over death. The muscular figure climbing effortlessly out of the grave, with his round dark eyes fixed on nothingness: filled with a fathomless vacancy and yet piercing the beholder with uncanny force.

He lives, but his mother dies. That was what it looked like. Her friends around her in Van der Goes's picture only emphasise the solitude of the central figure, lost in her blue-grey mantle of existlessness.

W.H. Auden had been to Belgium, and he wrote a memorable poem, *Musée des Beaux Arts*. I remembered that now too. Auden must have seen Breughel's painting of the Fall of Icarus. From this picture he drew the conclusion that 'they were never wrong, the Old Masters.' They understood the solitude and separation in which we all live, engrossed in our own lives. The soldiers around the grave are asleep when Christ steps from his tomb. The ship that must have seen the boy Icarus falling from the sky sails calmly on. The dying Virgin seems indifferent to her friends, and at a great distance from them.

For all their beauty and memorability all these pictures went out of my head when I was in my house again. Iris, too, was not there; neither as she once was nor as she had become. Not even Iris on her deathbed, whom I saw in my mind's eye so many times every day, and whom I had felt I was seeing in the picture. They had all gone, and with them had gone the memory of love.

There remained that Belgian sausage, long, hard and weighty. It brought to mind Mella's pie. And our Great Pie of long ago, the first that had gone to Pieland.

*

There was a sudden loud knocking on the door. The bell had still not been fixed. It was quite early, just after eight in the morning.

It was three weeks now since I had got home. My state of agitated vulnerability had again become normal. I had taken to locking the doors as I had locked them in Iris's time. Now I locked them to try to feel secure in my own house.

Memory, like a cancer, had returned to eat me up. I welcomed it too. Where should I be without it?

I hated even looking out of the window. What calamity was I expecting? There was nothing, good or bad, to expect.

Brussels had been a dream. But I still saw so clearly the Angel of Death and her smile – although now there was only the certainty of tiresomeness, in all its leaden forms. The widower's curse. Trouble would come. It would probably come in the predictable form of a helping hand. Trouble was a friendly knock on the door. So was fear.

How exciting and yet how full of fear the cinema had once been! The explorers or the soldiers were tiptoeing through the jungle. I used to feel a kind of despair on their behalf. Both excitement and hope-lessness. In spite of all the precautions they took, the dreadful thing was bound to happen. Indians would ambush them; the bearded tribesmen would rush out. I always knew the good guys would win in the end, but that was not the point. Far, far worse was the dreadful certainty that they would soon be in bad trouble.

Those joys and terrors were long ago. Meanwhile the house was decaying around me; in a terminal state, as if it, too, suffered from the cancer of recall.

And then there came the knocking again, like the knocking on the gate in *Macbeth*. Trouble from somebody. Not likely to be Indians or tribesmen. Something worse than that.

CHAPTER NINE

The Return of Mella and Margot

And yet probably just a parcel. Most likely six of Iris's novels in Turkish. Or Japanese. They arrived regularly, adding to the confusion of objects on the floor – no room for them anywhere else – but I welcomed their arrival none the less, and even looked inside them with curiosity; as if Iris's words might have taken on another meaning in this unknown tongue, and reveal to me something new and wonderful. Not about the incomprehensible language in which they now found themselves, but about Iris herself.

I remembered the moment, about three months before she died, when the same thing happened. The banging on the door had come at about the same time. Iris was asleep, and I was reading in bed beside her. I had the typewriter on my lap, but at that good time of the morning I used to indulge myself in a page or two of a familiar book, some old favourite which I could then look forward to reading more of over supper.

It was the peaceful time, from about six till nine in the morning, before I had to get up and try to persuade her to drink tea, eat porridge … Then the day's troubles began. How much I missed them now.

Through the glass in the front door I saw, on that occasion, the delivery man with his big parcel. I made signs for him to leave it on the step outside. That was because the door was locked on the inside. It had to be.

Miming his regrets the delivery man indicated through the glass that he had to have a signature. I had already realised I had forgotten to bring the key down; that was why I had signed to him to leave the parcel. The key was in my trouser pocket, but I had not got my trousers on. Only shirt and dressing-gown.

187

I stole upstairs, got the key without waking Iris, and let the parcel in. He was a nice man, I remembered, and we had a moment or two's chat about the weather, although I was rather conscious at the open door of my trouserless state. When I got upstairs again Iris had woken up and the peaceful part of the morning was over.

These former things were vivid in my head as I went to the front door to let in what at that time of the morning – barely eight o'clock – could only be the post or a parcel. So vivid was my memory of that earlier occasion that I found myself wondering, as I had often done at the time, why it was that Iris so much preferred to be left as she was: always dressed, always unwashed. Could it have been because *I really preferred it too*, in my own case, I mean; and Iris was expressing, in some strange way, a kind of sympathy and solidarity with me? Was it an aspect of our closeness, one that had now come fully out, fully into its own?

However that was, I felt sure that Iris was pleased not to be bothered and cared for when it came to clothes and hygiene. She could do as she wished, and as she preferred, just as if she had not been an invalid and a patient but a normal person. At the time I really felt that she was happy and pleased about that. She seemed to show it sometimes by smiling, as if understandingly, by stroking and caressing me. And as I went to the door at that moment I could feel her presence, as if I were still holding her hand.

At Alzheimer meetings since then I had made the point that it might be better for the patient, and for the carer too, just to let things go in this same way. Better all round in fact. And I had felt pleased and honoured when Dr Jacoby summed up at one of these meetings by agreeing that it could be a good solution. He had seen so many cases, in families looking after an Alzheimer patient, of over-insistence on cleanliness and tidiness. It could cause stress and exhaustion all round. Family friction as well, in a situation that was already quite bad enough.

I was lost among these thoughts – quite bemused. I saw the kindly face of Dr Jacoby when he used to visit us, and Iris rushed to meet him like a child, smiling all over her face.

Lost in the past, I stooped down to undo the bolt on the front door. It must be the parcel man, with six novels in Turkish, Hungarian, or Japanese. I should have to sign for them. I hadn't even looked through the glass to see who was there.

It was not six of Iris's novels in Turkish or in Japanese. It was Mella. And it was Margot. Both together.

They stood shoulder to shoulder, smiling at me.

Mella looked rather well. Hair tidy, almost shining. Face perhaps more eager and expectant than happy, but cheerful anyway. Margot, as usual, a big, calm, smiling presence.

I gaped at them. They looked solid enough, like the great Belgian sausage, which by now I had successfully eaten. But were they really just phantoms of my brain? A brain distracted by living in this house, among all its fears and fancies and anxieties?

As I gazed at them, with my mouth no doubt hanging foolishly open, I had the grotesque thought, certainly born of the Alzheimer meetings and our discussions there, that Mella might be expecting me to wash her, as Iris had not done. It had been pleasant and peaceful not to bother Iris with fuss about hygiene. But perhaps Mella would be more demanding now? She might *insist* on being washed?

'Oh, do come in,' I heard myself saying.

As I uttered the words I had a vision of escape. I would go back to Brussels. I would seek out the Angel of Death. Together we would fly to a distant, tropical country. The Angel would occupy herself with some theatrical enterprise. I would support and assist her. In the warm evenings we would sit together, our work done, listening to the tree-frogs and smelling the heavy scent of dark petals and Zambezi mud ...

We would be calm. We would be happy.

*

'We've just this moment got here from Heathrow,' announced Margot.

There was something gushing and unfamiliar about the way she

189

spoke, as if her relationship with Mella, whatever it was or had become, had changed her whole personality. Perhaps mine had changed too? Other people were said to notice such a thing more than one did oneself.

Margot was now babbling something about Barcelona. Why Barcelona?

I was locked eye to eye with Margot. As we gazed tautly at each other, revelation came to me abruptly. Margot was afraid of Mella. That was why they were here. Wherever they had been together, Barcelona or somewhere, Margot had managed to bring her here now in order to get rid of her. She was afraid of Mella. Indeed it looked as if she had come positively to hate her. And to think I had once found myself afraid of Margot!

How confusing it all was. I remembered in a benumbed way, and hardly even with astonishment, that it was Mella who had said she hated Margot. How could one know where one was with them? My own part in the trio, such as it was, seemed to have shrunk away to nothing. That should have given me relief and satisfaction, and yet I realised gloomily that it did not. I might think I wanted to get away from both of them; but that did not mean I wanted now to be left out of whatever was going on between them.

'Well, I must be getting along,' said Margot. Her voice had a ghastly jauntiness; her eyes met mine and looked quickly away. Easy for her to talk, but would the gangster let her go?

'Goodness knows what's been happening at home,' Margot went on. 'My precious animals must feel awfully neglected. Jimmy and George and the poor little donkey, and those hens you're so fond of, Johnny...'

Her voice trailed away and she seized her bag. Mella glanced incuriously from one of us to the other.

Should I try to get away, not with the Angel of Death, but with Margot? It was a terrible prospect, fond as I might be not only of Margot but of her hens, those great speckly monsters. And the poor little donkey, come to that. And even Jimmy and George, that clapped-out couple who wandered all day about the paddock with sad equine patience. No, I couldn't face it. Besides, there was no indication at all that Margot needed a companion in her getaway.

Voluble in her goodbyes and good wishes, 'You *must* come! – both of you – *any* time,' Margot was out of the door. She waved vigorously without turning round. A moment later a car started.

'Well, that's a relief,' said Mella. 'Bloody woman.'

*

Was she coming out in her true colours now? Did anyone have any true colours? The bloody woman had been of great service to her – she had wanted to be. Mella had none the less exploited her. Said once that she hated her. Had been all over Margot before that, and presumably after it too. Free trip to Barcelona? Why had they wanted to go to Barcelona, of all places?

With a timing that seemed uncanny Mella answered that question. 'I have this thing about Gaudí,' she remarked airily. 'Margot likes him too, or says she does. I really couldn't go on living without seeing the Sagrada Familia.'

What was all this then? But Mella no longer surprised me; she just depressed and exhausted me. She made me feel I never wanted to see anybody ever again.

Had I ever really known anybody, except Iris? Had I ever really known her? *Yes, of course I had.*

But perhaps Mella was unusually unknowable. Even Margot's behaviour had begun to startle me. Was it just that I had no idea nowadays, in my solitary state, how people could be expected to behave? Or what they wanted, or how they lived? None of these things had seemed to matter before, or even to exist. When there had been just the two of us – Iris and me – everything and everybody made sense. Or if they didn't do so, it wasn't any business of mine.

I noticed an efficient-looking holdall, fat and well zipped, which had appeared beside the kitchen door. In the confusion all round it looked trim and determined. It looked as if it had come to stay.

How long ago it seemed since Mella had run away into the snow. And vanished.

Paying her bag no attention, Mella sauntered out of the kitchen. I heard her on the stairs. Probably she needed a pee, which was natural enough. Margot had been too precipitate to stop for one. All she had thought about was getting away. We had no lavatory on the ground floor, possibly the consequence, as Iris and I had sometimes speculated, of the house having been built by and for a pair of maiden ladies. We had no other evidence of the existence of those ladies – a gentle, retiring sort of couple? – but in those days we liked to imagine them.

Mella's voice floated down from upstairs, but I couldn't hear what she was saying. My house had suddenly become dreadfully, overpoweringly domesticated. All around me, in addition to the usual mess were faint but discernible traces of Mella's previous attempts at clearing things up, attempts so much more effective than Margot's. The latter, I remembered, had scarcely got going at all.

I continued to stand motionless, as if paralysed. Mella's voice was again audible from upstairs, with a rather more demanding note in it. She seemed to require my presence.

She was standing in the bedroom, holding a single sock in her hand. Her voice when she spoke was mild and explanatory, as if she were telling me something I ought to know about for my own good.

'Seventy per cent nylon thirty per cent wool is better, you know,' she said. 'This is a woollen sock, and look at the hole! The moths are in it too.'

This was yet another side to Mella. I preferred it. A dangerous, if not fatal, preference, as I quickly saw. She seemed relaxed and peace-loving, as if she had recently won a great victory. Against Margot no doubt? After that I was a simple assignment. She would have no trouble with me.

She was all kindness and benevolence now, prepared to let me off the delinquent sock. Men couldn't be expected to manage such things. They needed pork pies too, and other feminine favours.

I wondered vacantly what lies, or even truths, she had told Margot about our relations. And yet why should she bother? None the less I felt a little hurt at the idea of being left out. No doubt their own relationship, whatever it was, had absorbed them completely.

Then what had gone wrong? Something had. There was nothing 'feminist' about either of them, no suggestion of solidarity or a sisterhood that excluded men. Had that been why they quarrelled? If they had? Or was I just being inept and patronising? Whatever the truth of the matter it looked as if Margot was not prepared to tolerate Mella and her company a moment longer. She was desperate to get rid of her. Had that sudden trip to Spain, undertaken with an almost honeymoon gaiety, ended in a row? Was Margot through with Holy Families, and with Lame Ducks as well?

Was she longing now to get back to her real animals, to the hens, the ancient horses and the donkey?

With an effort I brought back my attention to Mella. She was a phenomenon not to be got rid of, at least not by me, and certainly not at this moment. How much I envied Margot! But there was nowhere I could escape to as she had just done.

'What about your flat?' I asked. 'Have you been back there yet?'

I knew she hadn't. Margot had said that they had this minute arrived from Heathrow, and Margot was a woman whose word could be trusted. Unlike me? Unlike Mella? Perhaps Mella and I were soulmates really? Two of a kind?

What about the lady porter, who had told me about Mella's flat? She had seemed a trustworthy woman, like Margot. It seemed certain that the flat existed, and that Mella occupied it. Then why hadn't the pair of them gone straight round there, instead of coming straight to me?

Grimly I thought I saw the reason. Margot wanted the job to be done properly. A handing-over ceremony, just as I remembered from the army, in which responsibility was formally transferred from one person to another. Margot was making sure that I didn't miss the point. Mella was going to be my problem from now on.

Margot might be honest, at least compared to Mella and me, but I could hardly believe that after a few days in Mella's company she could have continued to believe the waif-and-stray story. As an orphan of the storm she had been authentic enough, so that was indeed a sense in which I, too, had been deceived. What had she done then? Conquered Margot? Or rather reconquered her and bewitched her? In the end Margot had the sense to run for it, flee away home in her car.

But I *was* in my home. Or rather in my house. What was I to do now?

'Let me give you a lift,' I said. 'Back to your place.'

Mella said nothing and we continued to stand in the bedroom. Was it to be the centre of our lives from now on? I cast a despairing glance at the dishevelled bed, the books, my typewriter, the worn old rubber cushion that propped my back when I sat typing in bed. How purposeful and happy they all looked! How much I loved them and yearned to be back among them! The things of the house, which had always been there, and which I could rely on as I had once relied on Iris's presence. They were just as they had been early this morning, when I sat in bed reading. Should I ever be able to read there again?

Hypnotised by their familiar presence I hardly noticed that Mella had not replied to my suggestion. When she did so her words filled me with a renewal of all my alarms. And not just alarm. Despair.

'Oh,' she said, 'you mean my flat? I've given that up. I only had it by the month, and they were always bothering me about the rent. The landlord was terribly tiresome.' She dropped my sock on the floor.

'But what about all your things?' I cried, trying to keep the panic out of my voice.

'My things?' Mella said patiently. 'My things are all in my little bag. Downstairs. The flat was rented furnished, of course.'

She picked up the sock again and looked at it critically, sniffed at it, turned it inside out or right way round – I couldn't see which – and dropped it on the floor again.

'Not worth washing,' she said, comfortably, as if there were lots of things here that might be worth it, and which she would soon be giving herself the pleasure of attending to.

'I must have a pee,' she went on. 'Forgot about it when we landed.'

She wandered off in the direction of the bathroom.

Had I come to a decision without knowing it, ever since the pair of them appeared at the door? However that might be, this moment now was a revelation.

I must leave the house. I must leave it at once.

The mistake had been to cling on so desperately to my life there. It was the house itself, my widower's house, that was causing the trouble, however much I felt that I loved it, needed it, filled it with the consolations of the past. For Iris was no longer in it; Iris was no longer there, as she had been after her first death. She did not exist now except in my own mind, and even in my own mind her existence was purely notional.

I remembered – what a moment to remember it – the important concept on which she had made herself an expert when she worked at the Treasury during the war. 'Notional promotion *in absentia*.' Soldiers from the peacetime Civil Service were metaphysically promoted, in terms of their future pay and prospects, as if they were still doing their old jobs at home.

Now Iris was *in absentia*, and her notional existence was fading, dying, disappearing out of my head. Except at those moments of joy and grief, when involuntary memory released the real Iris to leap out and surprise me …

But she was not in the house. That was certain. Unanticipated moments of grief and joy, if they continued to come to me, could come anywhere.

The house had become like a fortification, as in the old days of military science. A dangerous place, because it attracted enemy shell-fire. *I must leave the house*. If I stayed I should never know the peace and quiet I thought I wanted. If I did want them. Whether I did or not, the solution was so obvious now that I felt exalted. As if I had been suddenly told I could fly.

My old terror of leaving the house since Iris died – my fear of going anywhere. How absurd those terrors and fears now seemed!

I must escape from my own house, just as Iris used to try to escape. And sometimes, if I had been careless, Iris had succeeded. In the unknown wilderness of dementia she, too, had felt that she must leave home. Somehow. Anyhow …

So the thing now, the only thing, was to get away. To imitate Iris. To follow in her footsteps.

I went quickly and quietly downstairs and picked up my coat, with my wallet in the pocket. I squeezed the front door shut behind me. How many times Iris and I had started out like this on our little walks together, except that in those days I had had to unlock the door before we could get out.

Should I lock it now, on the outside? Better not. Mella might hear me.

I closed the door carefully and quietly, and ran away.

CHAPTER TEN

Leaving Home

And so, in one sense, that was the end of it. The end of the story.

But the tale of the widower's house is not quite over.

I decided to take the train to London. Even the simple business of getting a ticket – simple maybe, but absurdly slow and tiresome – had been a purgatory since I had been on my own and compelled to go to London for some reason. Now it all paraded along with fabulous ease, as if I were indeed flying.

I had a credit card and money in my wallet. I had left home. I could do as I pleased.

But most of my fears came back as the little train rattled on its way to Reading. Where was I to go? Where could I stay? I might be able to fly, but somehow I couldn't face the thought of going to a London hotel.

In the old days Iris had a tiny flat, more of a 'pad' really, at the top of a very tall but rather gimcrack house in a Kensington square. Innumerable stairs. No lift. The floors at the top were so flimsy they creaked at the lightest tread, and Iris used to creep about in her socks for fear of disturbing the tenants below. But she loved it. It was useful for seeing her friends, and essential early on, when her mother was still alive. I loved it too on the occasions I went there, particularly at Christmas time, and on our periodic jaunts, when we bought food and wine in the Gloucester Road and had a long picnic.

Tall as the house was the plane trees in the square outside were even taller, and in summer their broad leaves, pale green against the black and yellow pattern of the trunk, looked in at our window.

After Iris died the pad was got rid of. I couldn't bear to go there; it was the reverse of my house. It was Iris's flat, and there she had lived her own life, seeing her friends all day, creeping back upstairs to bed in the evening. In the morning at seven or so I used to ring her, acting as an alarm clock, and I loved her sleepy, happy 'Wow Wow' as she answered the phone.

It would have been useful now as a jumping-off place. Now that I had left home. I felt about my house now as I had felt about the flat after Iris died.

But what should I do now? I had no idea.

And then suddenly I had. It was obvious: it stared me in the face, just as the need to escape had done.

I would ring up Audi and ask if I could come and stay for a bit in Lanzarote. She had said, very kindly, that I could come and stay if I wanted, but she had never pressed or bothered me about it.

I clutched at my coat pocket, the opposite side to my wallet. Her long phone number was written in my diary, along with others which I could not possibly have remembered, and, thank goodness, my diary was there. So why shouldn't I go now straight to Gatwick instead of to London, which I instinctively feared, and get a ticket and get on the first available flight? I knew there was an airport hotel; I had seen it the last time I had been away – ages ago it seemed.

I caught the train from Reading to Gatwick, and as I sat down a sort of jerk jumped up into my mouth.

Oh heavens! My passport!

My passport must be sitting back in the house. With Mella. Perhaps she had already found it. And confiscated it.

The train was crawling steadily towards Gatwick, towards freedom. But of what use was freedom without a passport? I sat there hopelessly. When it arrived I should have to get in another train and go back home. If Mella was still there, still occupying my house, and I was sure she would be, how was I to get at my passport?

Then I had another inspiration. The passport was a new one, a flimsy little red thing which had replaced the old stout blue-bound document 'requesting and requiring' all foreigners whatsoever to assist and befriend me as a subject of Her Majesty. Those fine resonant sentences had probably been dropped.

But what had happened, as I now recollected, was that at the time of our last visit to France, to Natasha Spender's cottage in Provence – Iris and I and Peter Conradi looking after us – I had travelled with a passport already out of date. We had sailed past the control in all innocence. The passport photo was glanced at and the document politely returned. But Peter had spotted the date on the way home; and this time we slunk guiltily past the official, who again hardly bothered with us.

But soon after that, and in the midst of all my other troubles, with Iris's condition getting worse every day, I had none the less remembered to apply for a new passport.

When the burglars came they had taken what money there was from the kitchen drawer, but not the new passport. Providentially: because I knew from hearsay that a stolen passport had considerable value. I felt deeply grateful to the burglars for not taking it. But in case they came again, or in case another lot of burglars visited me, I had taken the precaution of tucking the little passport into my wallet, where it fitted quite comfortably.

But was it still there?

Thank God, it was! It was still there because I had forgotten all about it. I felt I could face anything now. And to think that I might have gone tamely home, with the passport all the time in my wallet!

My luck held. The charter flight to Lanzarote turned out to be full that day, but there were two or three the day after. I was on the waiting list with a good chance of catching one of them. I managed to ring Audi.

It was still only three in the afternoon. The day dragged. I prowled restlessly about the little hotel room, lying on the bed and trying to relax, but then almost immediately getting up again. I felt sober now, with all the exaltation of leaving home quite gone.

Had it been a mean thing to leave Mella like that? Of course it had been a mean thing, but something had had to be done; I even felt a sneaking gratitude to Mella for forcing me to make up my mind. Thanks to her I had had no choice. Deliberately or unconsciously she must have thought that I would acquiesce in her annexation of the house, and of me too. I would helplessly accept a *fait accompli* and let her live with me, at least for the moment.

But no! Whatever she was, Mella wasn't like that. She wasn't a schemer, an adventuress, a woman who lived by the wits and the will. True, in that tense three-cornered situation with Margot I had seen her briefly as a gangster, holding a pistol to our heads. But come, the poor girl was more like an autumn leaf, fluttering from place to place, person to person, moment to moment. If I could have done more for her I might have felt more sorry for her – sorry, not guilty. But I knew I could only go on doing the same sort of thing – her coffee and biscuit, the tepid time in bed, the walk round the block.

Perhaps that would have been doing more for her? – all the 'more' of which I was capable? I actually felt now a twinge of nostalgia, of homesickness even, for what we used to do together. Was that the routine, and the kind of 'peace and quiet', which I had really wanted?

But was it what Mella wanted? It came over me again, as so often since I had been alone, that I seemed to know nothing about anybody. What about Margot? Her behaviour with Mella had surely been far from sensible. Had she, too, been blindly in search of a friend, a companion, a helpmate of some sort? Against all the loneliness and fear, the anxieties of being on one's own? She had been wrong about Mella, but how could she have been right? How could I have been right? I was still sure that Mella was not a bad person, not even a scheming person. But how did that help? It was not Mella's fault that she had this effect on the people she met, or rather on the people who found that they had met her.

I got up, wandered about, lay down again. I didn't even want a drink, let alone any dinner. I had begun to feel a more acute anxiety about Mella's activities. What was she doing now? Had she given up and gone away? Somehow that seemed too much to hope for.

As I prowled about my unresponsive little room at the airport hotel I tried to imagine what might be going on back in my house. I felt sure that Mella was still there, but what would she be up to? After all the agitations of the day, I couldn't remember my own phone number, but

I had had the forethought to write that down too, at the front of my diary.

The phone in the house rang and rang, and nobody answered it. But that did not reassure me. Obviously Mella, if Mella was lying there in wait, would not answer the phone. She would not wish to alert a caller, who might be a friend of mine, to what was going on in the house.

I stopped ringing, waited for an interval, and tried again. Still no reply.

Then it occurred to me to try my neighbour, who had the spare keys. Her number, too, was in my diary. She was a helpful, good-natured lady. I said that I was very sorry to bother her but I thought I might have left the back door unlocked, and I would be away for a day or two. I mentioned the visit of the burglars. Could she very kindly check that back door?

How would she deal with Mella, if Mella were still there? I told myself, and I was not being disingenuous, that my neighbour was the sort of person who enjoyed a challenge. She would enjoy, too, making a sensible and brisk response. I need not worry too much on her behalf, I thought, even though it was quite possible that Mella would find some way of attaching herself to my neighbour as she had initially done to Margot. Or was it more likely that my neighbour would accept Mella's presence sensibly and briskly, even if with some tacit disapproval? It was no business of hers if I kept a mistress in my house, who preferred not to answer the phone.

At last it was time to ring back. My neighbour sounded unsurprised. Yes, the back door had been open. She had locked it.

Another piece of undeserved good fortune. But relief was soon tempered by anxiety. For one thing, I should not have behaved as I had done towards Mella. I should have asked her firmly to leave, and softened firmness by offering to help her, although short of giving her money, which she did not seem to need, and would possibly have refused with indignation, I saw no material way in which I could be of use.

But another possibility was much more alarming. Suppose she had just popped out for a while to buy food? And perhaps arrange with a locksmith to change the keys of the house? Such reckless daring and bold initiative did not seem like Mella, but what did I know about Mella after all? I only knew that Margot, warm, sensible, open-hearted woman as she was, had decided that enough was enough where she and Mella were concerned, and had barnacled the girl back on to me.

During the night, which was interminable, I tried to do some of what used to be called 'straight thinking'. All my timidities and illusions now seemed crystal clear. But – thank goodness – by four in the morning it began to go all fuzzy in my mind. Dream images and objects came instead, although I knew that I was still awake. Mella entered the room. She looked like an owl, with a sharp beak and round accusing eyes. She brought with her, like a parcel, a piece of poetry – it must be from *Paradise Lost*.

> As when a Gryphon through the wilderness
> Pursues the Arimaspian ...

Who was this Arimaspian? I tried to ask Mella but she did not reply. She just looked at me with big, clear, yellow eyes.

*

'How's the Arimaspian this morning?'

Audi looked and sounded amused. I had told her the night before about the Arimaspian, and Mella, and leaving the house. I had been tired, and had talked a lot, and drunk a lot of red *rioja* wine. The flight to Lanzarote is never easy and always crowded, and it had been delayed.

But Audi looked as if something else was amusing her too; something about which I had not told her, something she must have deduced for herself.

It was a calm, tranquil morning. No wind for once. We could hear a hoopoe calling somewhere far off, and the neat cone of the mountain, pale in the sunlight, had a delicate cinnamon flush which spread into darker colours down its barren flanks.

Audi had listened with patient indulgence to the tale of my leaving home. Through the mistiness of a mild headache I thought over and over how Iris had sometimes escaped too; leaving dementia behind by leaving the house when I forgot to lock the door. When I found her, or when she came back, she wore a mysteriously mischievous but satisfied expression: as if she had found something, or seen some spectacle, about which she could not tell me, or anyone else.

Audi brought out our breakfast to the terrace, where I was contemplating the mountain and listening for the distant hoopoe. Though a good bit less than a thousand feet its shape somehow made it a mountain rather than a mere hill. It was restful to contemplate, while from time to time laying a hand on my brow. It must have been this that occasioned Audi's amusement at the appearance and demeanour of the Arimaspian. Had he also, I wondered, taken refuge in the bottle from thoughts of his pursuer?

After I had told her about him the previous evening, and about my dream, Audi had gone to find her copy of Milton – an annotated one. I had no idea where the Arimaspian was, although I felt that he was somewhere in *Paradise Lost*. With quiet persistence Audi, one of nature's scholars, tracked him down as we continued to sit chatting and drinking our wine. There he was, in Book II, a one-eyed Scythian tribesman who stole the Gryphon's gold, and was implacably pursued over hill and dale, through plains and deserts, by that fabulous beast, half eagle and half lion.

Was Mella like a Gryphon? Poor Mella – I could hardly believe in her existence now, whether as a real girl or as a legendary monster who might still be pursuing me. And yet Mella, unlike the fabulous Gryphon, did exist, and I had escaped from her. Or was it rather that I had abandoned her? In any case it was unfair to turn her into a monster. But dreams are unfair, as much as are the lives and habits they reflect.

Should I not have reasoned with Mella, compromised and discussed, above all made some attempt to find out about her? She had never seemed to want to talk about herself; but then, I had never given her any encouragement to do so. I had thought only of my own state, and what I had seen as my own needs. Being a widower had indeed turned me into a monster of egoism, just as I had once suspected.

Of course it was open to me to feel, if I felt like it, that widowers had a natural right to be monsters of egoism. Widows too, come to that. But what about Margot? Had she not done her best for Mella, out of kindness as well as out of her own needs, whatever they were? Mella, it was true, had told her a lot of lies, many more than she had bothered to tell me.

I could tell myself now that I had had to abandon Mella – nothing else would have worked. It might well be true, though I didn't like the taste of it. Was I developing a conscience at long last? Was that the trouble? In any case I poured it all out to Audi.

She had listened patiently, and finally said that without knowing either of these two ladies she could hardly give an opinion. But that was reassurance enough, and a great and somehow comic restfulness seemed to come over us while we talked. Perhaps all my problems and troubles as a widower were not so serious after all?

Perhaps it was just the red Spanish wine, but it really did seem as if anxieties and loss had miraculously taken their departure.

*

One night a week later we went out into the garden after supper. Audi was going to show me the night-flowering cactus, which she hoped might just have come into bloom. There was a crescent moon, but it was very dark, and she took my hand to steer us through the *picon*, velvet black in the darkness, which rose and fell in miniature dunes among the acacias and the wizened lemon trees.

Then Audi switched on her torch, revealing a ghost-like apparition, a dark pillar twelve feet high and covered in spectral white flowers. They blossomed, she said, for a single night: by morning they would have disappeared.

We stood hand in hand in silence while the light from Audi's torch stole about among the gigantic ghost-blooms, bowing and shaking in the night wind. Gazing at them, spellbound, I was back at the beginning of the year. The flowers were like a dance of the blessed spirits. I didn't believe in blessed spirits; but I believed that Iris was with me once more, joining us and making three with us in the warm breath of the night.

A moment later she seemed still closer. A huge moth from Africa flew out of the darkness above our heads and hovered in the torchlight round the flowers. I remembered Iris's strange genius for summoning to her those frail creatures of the night, succouring them and setting them on the way they should go. Once in a hotel at dinner-time the waiters had been trying to knock such a moth down with their napkins, as it flitted to and fro over the heads of the diners. But it flew down straight to Iris's hand, and she carried it to a window, and we watched it fly safely away into the darkness.

Audi and I talked for a long time that night, and on the days that followed, and as we talked Iris came always closer to both of us. Grief may have been difficult to live with, but much worse had been its aftermath, and all the new problems and difficulties it had brought. Now all these had vanished, and Iris was here, the three of us together as we had so often been together in the past.

Audi knew this, I realised. And it soon became clear that she knew – as well as I had begun to do – the real reason why I had come to her, and why I had abandoned the widower's house.